FOUL DEEDS AND SUSPICIOUS DEATHS AROUND WORCESTER

TRUE CRIME FROM WHARNCLIFFE
Foul Deeds and Suspicious Deaths Series

Barking, Dagenham & Chadwell Heath
Barnsley
Bath
Bedford
Birmingham
Black Country
Blackburn and Hyndburn
Bolton
Bradford
Brighton
Bristol
Cambridge
Carlisle
Chesterfield
Colchester
Coventry
Croydon
Derby
Dublin
Durham
Ealing
Folkestone and Dover
Grimsby
Guernsey
Guildford
Halifax
Hampstead, Holborn and St Pancras
Huddersfield
Hull

Leeds
Leicester
Lewisham and Deptford
Liverpool
London's East End
London's West End
Manchester
Mansfield
More Foul Deeds Birmingham
More Foul Deeds Chesterfield
More Foul Deeds Wakefield
Newcastle
Newport
Norfolk
Northampton
Nottingham
Oxfordshire
Pontefract and Castleford
Portsmouth
Rotherham
Scunthorpe
Southend-on-Sea
Staffordshire and The Potteries
Stratford and South Warwickshire
Tees
Warwickshire
Wigan
York

OTHER TRUE CRIME BOOKS FROM WHARNCLIFFE

A-Z of Yorkshire Murder
Black Barnsley
Brighton Crime and Vice 1800-2000
Durham Executions
Essex Murders
Executions & Hangings in Newcastle
    and Morpeth
Norfolk Mayhem and Murder

Norwich Murders
Strangeways Hanged
The A-Z of London Murders
Unsolved Murders in Victorian and
    Edwardian London
Unsolved Norfolk Murders
Unsolved Yorkshire Murders
Yorkshire's Murderous Women

Please contact us via any of the methods below for more information or a catalogue.
WHARNCLIFFE BOOKS
47 Church Street – Barnsley – South Yorkshire – S70 2AS
Tel: 01226 734555 – 734222 Fax: 01226 734438
E-mail: enquiries@pen-and-sword.co.uk
Website: www.wharncliffebooks.co.uk

Foul Deeds & Suspicious Deaths Around

WORCESTER

ANNE BRADFORD

Series Editor
Brian Elliott

Wharncliffe Books

First published in Great Britain in 2008 by
Wharncliffe Local History
an imprint of
Pen & Sword Books Ltd
47 Church Street
Barnsley
South Yorkshire
S70 2AS

ISBN 978 1 84563 0669

Typeset in 11/13pt Plantin by
Mac Style, Nafferton, East Yorkshire

Printed and bound in the UK by
CPI

Pen & Sword Books Ltd incorporates the imprints of Pen & Sword
Aviation, Pen & Sword Maritime, Pen & Sword Military, Wharncliffe Local
History, Pen and Sword Select, Pen and Sword Military Classics and
Leo Cooper.

For a complete list of Pen & Sword titles please contact
PEN & SWORD BOOKS LIMITED
47 Church Street, Barnsley, South Yorkshire, S70 2AS, England
E-mail: enquiries@pen-and-sword.co.uk
Website: www.pen-and-sword.co.uk

Contents

Dedication

Dedicated to the memory of Barrie Roberts, with whom I have worked on several books since 1994.

Barrie was a former criminal lawyer who specialized in the analysis of evidence. He was an internationally published writer, having written six Sherlock Holmes pastiches, several modern mystery novels and innumerable articles for the international press. We should have been working together on this book, but he died on 11 June 1997.

Anne Bradford

Acknowledgements

The chapter on Bella of the Wych Elm was written entirely by David Taylor, an expert on the subject and Chairman of Parasearch, an investigative paranormal society. David has also drawn the relevant illustrations.

The information for the Flitch of Bacon murder at Foxlydiate and the murder of PC Davies in Wythall has been provided by Alan Foxall, Redditch author and historian.

The death of a hop-picker in Kidderminster has been based on information provided by Alan Lauder of Kidderminster Ghost Walks.

The chapter on the lovers' pact in Redditch and Northfield has been based on information from Maurice Clarke.

All photographs of contemporary scenes have been taken by John Bradford.

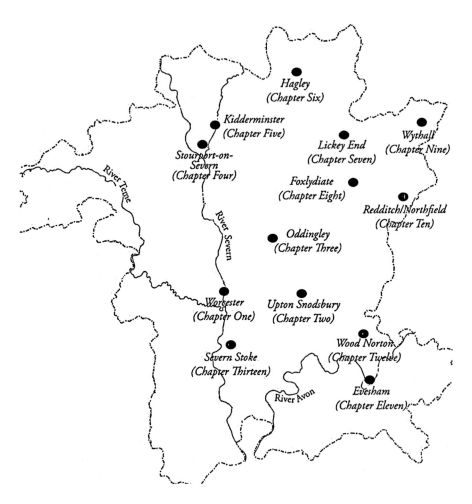

Map of Worcestershire, showing the sites of the murders described in this book. Not to scale.

Preface

Many of us who live here in Worcestershire believe this to be the finest county in England. It is a county of fertile farmland and tiny villages, and except for the flat Evesham plain, which is famous for its fruit and vegetables, of gentle green hills. Along the western side of the county run the nine miles of the Malvern Hills which rise to nearly 1,400 feet and inspired Elgar and Piers Plowman among other composers and writers. Of navigable rivers, the Avon crosses the county from east to west, the Teme comes from the west and joins the Severn at Powick near Worcester, while the River Severn runs from north to south, through Worcester, on the western side. At a time when the most reliable transport was by river, the Severn was the main artery of the county; now the M5, which roughly follows the same course, has taken over this function.

Some Worcestershire towns have been of national, even international, fame – Kidderminster for its carpets, Redditch for its needles, Bromsgrove for its nails, Droitwich for its salt. Many of the smaller towns, such as Evesham, Pershore, Bewdley, Great Malvern, Stourport-on-Severn and Upton-on-Severn attract many tourists. The largest towns are Worcester and Redditch. The ancient cathedral and the fine buildings give Worcester an attractive elegance. As for Redditch, its origins lie in the foundation of Bordesley Abbey in 1138. It was designated a new town in 1963 and the planners were at great pains to create a town with a wealth of greenery.

Those who now live in Worcestershire are amazed to hear of the county's turbulent past. In 1596 the Bishop of Worcester wrote to Lord Cecil that Worcestershire was as dangerous a place as any he knew. Until the seventeenth century a large part of the county was primeval forest, the haunt of outlaws and highwaymen. Villainy was endemic: whole families were

The view across Worcester from Fort Royal, built for the Battle of Worcester 1651. The Garibaldi (see Chapter 1) is at its foot.

sometimes slain and houses burnt after nightfall. The existing rolls for Worcestershire, covering only a few years in the 1300s, give a long list of murders. Most of them were committed on the highways by footpads.

Not only did the inhabitants of Worcestershire live in fear of outlaws, the early history of the county was that of piratical raids from the Irish, the Welsh and the Vikings from Norway and Denmark. In 1041 the Vikings swept up the River Severn, robbed the city and sacked the early cathedral. Legend tells that one of the Vikings tried to make off with the great Sanctus bell that rang for services, but it was too heavy for him, so he lagged behind his companions and was caught by the townsfolk. They flogged him to death and nailed a piece of his skin to the door of the cathedral.

For several decades following 1017 the Danes ruled a large part of England, including Worcestershire, and the citizens of Worcester rose in rebellion against the heavy taxes they imposed. They attacked the two tax collectors sent to enforce payment. The officials ran to the safety of the cathedral, but the mob chased and killed them. In reprisal, the king sent an army which spent four days burning the city to the ground and making off with anything of value.

Because of Worcestershire's position in the heart of England it was important strategically. It served as a base for military operations against mid and south Wales, and it was on a direct line of communication between London and Ludlow. Whoever controlled Worcestershire held the line of the River Severn. Worcestershire folk therefore suffered badly in the civil wars. The various armies were often ill-disciplined and hungry, so that looting and pillaging was common throughout the county.

The war between King Stephen and Empress Matilda began in 1139 and lasted for about fourteen years. At that time, Worcester was owned by a great warlord, Hugh de Waleran. First he fought for Matilda, so that King Stephen's army sacked Worcester city. Then he changed sides so that Matilda's army sacked Worcester. Matilda ruled for two years, when there was total anarchy throughout England.

Another civil war arose in 1264 for which Evesham is famous. Simon de Montfort decided that Henry III had too much authority and persuaded some barons to join him to depose the king. Simon camped at Evesham in 1265, believing that he was safe in the loop of the river, while he waited for his son to join him. Unfortunately, his son had already been defeated at Kenilworth. Advancing towards de Montfort were not reinforcements but the king's army. De Montfort saw that he was trapped and exclaimed, 'May God have mercy on our souls for our bodies are theirs.' Historians calculate that 4,000 died that day, including de Montfort and his son. However, he is now honoured for staking a first claim for democracy.

Three centuries later, Worcestershire became a political hotbed. The gentry refused to convert to Henry VIII's Church of England. In 1605 a plot was devised that shocked England and is remembered to this day. A group of well-bred young men planned to blow up the Houses of Parliament, kill the king and 300 leading Protestants. Among the conspirators were the Lyttletons of Hagley Hall, the Habingtons of Hindlip Hall, the Throckmortons of Coughton Court (just over the border in Warwickshire) and the Wyntours of Huddington Court.

Nearly forty years later the first Civil War of 1642–6 erupted, with Royalists fighting Parliamentarians. The first and last battles of this war took place in the Worcester area. The River Teme joins the Severn three miles outside Worcester at Powick, and it was here that a contingent of Parliamentarians and Royalists accidentally met in 1642. Some fifty Parliamentarians were killed, wounded or drowned and nearly every Royalist officer was injured in some way.

By 1646 the Royalists had been defeated. Charles I was beheaded in 1649, but two years later his eldest son, Charles Stuart, raised an army, chiefly from Scotland, and attempted to regain the throne. This led to the great Battle of Worcester of 1651. Some of the fiercest fighting took place inside the city, especially in and around Sidbury Gate. The *Garibaldi Inn* was later built on this very site and it was here that, in 1925, the licensee and his family were murdered by the friendly local police constable.

Chroniclers reckoned that of the 15,000 men of the Scottish army, 3,000 had been killed, 10,000 taken prisoner and 2,000 were scattered fugitives. The Parliamentarians under Oliver Cromwell were victorious, but Charles Stuart managed to escape and returned in 1660 to become King Charles II.

This was an age when men were prepared to die for their beliefs, and our earliest murder, covering the persecution of the Quakers, dates back to the time of Oliver Cromwell. A century and a half later, religion was still important and the local vicar or rector was still one of the most influential men in the community. At Oddingley, the rector came up against a self-styled elder of the village, Captain Evans, with disastrous results.

Right up until the middle of the twentieth century, the rigid code of ethics imposed by the Church governed society – and was possibly responsible for the infanticides described in the last chapter of this book. Perhaps it was also the underlying cause of the suicide pact between Harold Merry and Joyce Dixon, where Joyce was under pressure from her mother because she was going out with a married man. Whether society has swung in the opposite direction and is now too liberal is debatable.

Most of our murders occur between 1832 and 1925. The civil wars had passed, but life was still hard, difficult and often brutal, especially for the working classes. One of the greatest changes of this period was the advance of the Industrial Revolution. Industry became mechanized and people moved from farms or homesteads into large factories. The population of Worcestershire increased from 146,441 in 1801 to 488,355 in 1901, chiefly in the towns. Richard Heming, who was involved in the assassination of Reverend Parker, had moved from pretty little Bredon to Droitwich town. Moses Shrimpton, who assassinated PC Davies at Wythall, was born in the little village of Long Crendon, but his family were needle-makers and found it necessary to move to the factories of Redditch. Like other hastily built towns of that time, Redditch was described by the Medical Officer of Health in 1875 as a place where 'Sanitary conditions had been almost entirely sacrificed to cheap and imperfect construction'.

Young folk today have difficulty visualizing life in those times. There was no electricity – no television, no washing machine, no freezers, and no hairdryers. Lighting was by a candle, oil lamp or, later, a fragile gas mantle. You made your own entertainment. The 'wireless' did not arrive until the 1920s. Water was from a well or a pump, usually outside in the yard. At Upton Snodsbury, a track used by local women to get to the brook to do their washing ran past the cottage of Palmer's mother. Transport was by horse or horse-drawn vehicle. There was no car in which to take the injured gamekeeper of Wood Norton to the surgeon; instead the head gamekeeper put his horse in a trap. Bicycles appeared only in the late 1800s and affordable motor cars were not available until the 1920s.

As late as the 1880s, half the population could not read. The Church provided Sunday Schools and a few free schools, but, on the whole, there was no need to learn. Books were expensive, newspapers were few and far between and as family members rarely moved out of a village there was no need to write letters. Towards the end of the 1800s, education became a 'hot potato' for the government. The Education Act of 1870 brought in compulsory education, but it was not until 1891 that school fees were reduced or abolished. Many of our criminals could not read. Joseph and Samuel Boswell of Wood Norton had to dictate their letters from prison. Important evidence arose from the fact that Giles Hunt of Upton Snodsbury could not read.

People worked long hours: as late as 1901 a factory act stated that young persons were to work no longer than sixty-six hours per week. Wages were insufficient to feed and clothe the large families people went in for in those days. A large number of children were a necessity, not a luxury. You needed them to look after you in your old age, and you had to reconcile yourself to the loss of a child or two from measles, whooping cough, scarlet fever, diphtheria, pneumonia and other diseases that are almost unheard of today. A fifth of all babies died before their first birthday. Perhaps it was the death of Harold Merry's eldest daughter from diphtheria that was the underlying cause of his disastrous affair with Joyce Dixon after many years of happy marriage.

Unemployment benefit arrived as late as 1911, and then it was derisory. Old age pensions were not introduced until 1908, and were not paid until the age of 70. They were means-tested, and if you did qualify you received somewhere between ten and twenty-five pence a week. By 1925 they had risen to the grand sum of 50 pence a week. Until 1834, the Poor Law worked as a welfare state in miniature, but in 1834 the 'New Poor Law Amendment Act' swept away the Poor Laws and replaced them with a national system for dealing with the relief of poverty based on the dreaded Union Workhouse. The hop-picker who was killed in Kidderminster came from Walsall Union workhouse, where her alcoholic husband was still living.

A great divide separated the working and the upper classes, glimpsed in the 1707 tragic events at Upton Snodsbury and those of 1889 at Wood Norton. While the wives struggled to 'make do and mend' by, for example, cutting a torn sheet down the centre and sewing the two good edges together, the husbands were sometimes off trespassing and poaching, snaring a rabbit or two on a private estate. Small wonder that a fifth of all crimes that came before the courts was associated with poaching.

Workers often sought solace in drink. Samuel Middleton in Foxlydiate killed his wife in a drunken rage. Moses Shrimpton had visited more than one pub before he knifed the constable at Wythall. The poachers at Wood Norton were heavy drinkers; so were the perpetrators of the Upton Snodsbury crimes. William Lightband of Areley Kings admits that he drifted into bad company and spent his wages on drink. Perhaps the two unsolved murders at Bromsgrove and Kidderminster were also fuelled by drink.

Wartime hit Worcestershire again in 1939, and three of our murders come from this period. It was a time of imminent danger, of shortages and rationing, of the blackout, of working all day then going to voluntary work at night. It has been suggested that Bella, found in the wych-elm at Hagley, was a spy. Large buildings were adapted as billets for army use and for workers brought into the area. The hospital complexes at Bromsgrove were taken over first by British, then American casualties. Florrie Porter was killed here by an American officer by the name of Hal. Every available factory in the county was involved in war work of some kind or another. Harold Merry was moved to war work at the Austin factory, where he met Joyce Dixon.

A comforting thought is that most of these murders would not have occurred today. We live in comparatively peaceful times. There is no longer any disgrace in becoming an unmarried mother, and infanticides have virtually died out. Syphilis can be treated with drugs. Police constables no longer wander alone through lonely lanes. Workhouses have been abandoned and replaced by Social Services. An even more comforting thought is that the two unsolved murders, those of the hop-picker in Kidderminster and Bella of the wych-elm in Hagley, would probably have been solved with technological advances such as DNA. All these factors help to keep the crime rate low in Worcestershire, so that the county is not only beautiful but safe for its residents.

CHAPTER 1

The *Garibaldi* and the Rubber Gloves – Worcester

All murders are tragic events, bringing a life to a sudden, and often brutal, end. The lives of two families are shattered, those of the victim and those of the murderer. The horror can also reverberate to include many innocent people, for example, the two schoolboys cycling to school at Lickey End who had the unpleasant experience of finding a body (Chapter 7); Mrs Hassall's spotless house at Foxlydiate accidentally burning to the ground with the victim (Chapter 8); or the maid at Upton Snodsbury who ran to help her mistress and was killed (Chapter 2).

The murders at the *Garibaldi Inn* of 1925 were particularly tragic. One reason is that they involved a small child; another is that they were murders that should not have occurred. The murderer had been discharged from the navy on medical grounds, so why was he admitted to the police force? And again, it was so near – only a couple of decades – to the medical advances that would have prevented the tragedy.

The A44 from Pershore and Evesham approaches Worcester from the south-east, and as it nears the centre of the city it becomes known as 'Sidbury'. The gates of the city were here and, in 1651, this is where some of the fiercest fighting of the Battle of Worcester took place. A plaque on the bridge of the Worcester and Birmingham canal commemorates the event. Just before the canal bridge is a narrow one-way street, Wyld's Lane. On its western side, near the Sidbury end, was once an inn, known as the *Garibaldi*. The name was changed to the *Lamplighter*, then, in 1996, to the *Welcome Inn*. Perhaps the owners thought that a change of name would help folk to forget its terrible past.

At seven o'clock in the morning on Friday, 27 November 1925, Mrs Hardwick, the cleaning lady, went round to the

Garibaldi. The first strange thing was that the front door was open – no one had locked it. In the bar the till was lying on the ground and there was a quantity of copper and other coins scattered about, together with discs for the automatic machines. Everything was deathly quiet. She went upstairs to the licensee's 6-year-old-girl, Joan, who was fast asleep. Joan woke up when Mrs Hardwick entered the room and they exchanged a few words. She peeped into the baby's room, where 2-year-old Bobby appeared to be sleeping peacefully, face down in his cot. Of the licensees, Mr and Mrs Laight, there was no sign.

Ernest George Elton Laight had only been the licensee of the *Garibaldi* for seven months. Before then he had been a barber with a shop in New Street. He was 32 years of age and grew up in Worcester, a bright lad, keen on sports, especially football. When he left school he became a hairdresser but enlisted during the First World War and fought in France. During the war he married a local girl, Dolly Tolley. Trade at the *Garibaldi* was dwindling when he took it over, but he was an amiable man, open and friendly, and by November the *Garibaldi* was booming.

Mrs Hardwick decided to get help. She knocked up two nearby residents of Wyld's Lane. One of them, Mr Oram, had a look round: there was still no sign of the Laights. Seeing a door that led from the kitchen into the cellar, he went down the steps. He later described his reaction to the sight that awaited him as 'stricken a bit'.

He saw Mr Laight lying on the floor, outstretched. Then he saw another body lying face downwards, which he thought at first was another man. Part of the clothing was burned so that the buttocks were exposed and charred. The floor was covered with pieces of burned paper. Someone had evidently tried to burn the bodies. He rushed upstairs and found the baby stretched out in his cot, also dead. Of the Laight family, only the little girl was alive.

Police Constable Knight was the first to arrive, at a quarter to eight, followed by Dr Walpole, the pathologist, and Detective Sergeant Fisher. In the kitchen was a cash box containing only fifteen sixpenny pieces. In a cupboard in the baby's room was an empty cash box. The average takings at the *Garibaldi* were about £30 a week. Mr Laight had last cashed up on the 9th,

The *Welcome Inn,* formerly known as the *Garibaldi Inn,* immediately after its closure.

and so there should have been about £80 in the boxes. On a table in the kitchen were five bottles of spirits, four of which had been opened and a little taken from each. On the top of the cellar steps was a pair of rubber gloves.

Rumours spread like wildfire. Mr Oram thought they had been poisoned, as the baby had no signs of injury and in the darkness and chaos of the cellar he could see no blood.

Little Joan was taken to stay with Mrs Laight's mother, who kept the *Green Man* on a busy road, the Tything, a few streets away. The grandmother had remarried a Mr Harrison and it was he who identified the bodies. Mr Laight's mother was in Australia.

Dr Walpole immediately began a post-mortem examination. Mr Laight's body showed signs of scorching and there was a bullet in his chest that had gone through his heart and lung. The second body turned out to be that of Mrs Laight, who had both burns and abrasions, as if she had been dragged across the floor. There was a bullet at the lower end of her

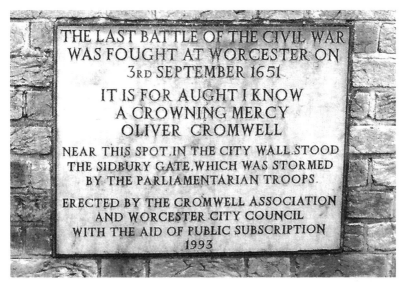

THE LAST BATTLE OF THE CIVIL WAR
WAS FOUGHT AT WORCESTER ON
3RD SEPTEMBER 1651

IT IS FOR AUGHT I KNOW
A CROWNING MERCY
OLIVER CROMWELL

NEAR THIS SPOT, IN THE CITY WALL, STOOD
THE SIDBURY GATE, WHICH WAS STORMED
BY THE PARLIAMENTARIAN TROOPS.

ERECTED BY THE CROMWELL ASSOCIATION
AND WORCESTER CITY COUNCIL
WITH THE AID OF PUBLIC SUBSCRIPTION
1993

Plaque on the wall of a bridge near Wyld's Lane.

sternum (breastbone), penetrating her heart and lung. The baby had a fractured skull and had been hit with a heavy object. At 3.30 pm Dr Walpole announced that the couple had died of gunshot wounds.

Repairs were being carried out to the road outside and a watchman had been on duty all night, but he had neither heard nor seen anything.

A Surprising Suspect
About the same time that the cleaner, Mrs Hardwick, was fetching her neighbours to search the *Garibaldi Inn*, Police Constable Herbert Burrows was coming off duty to have breakfast. He wandered over to see his colleague, Constable Devey, who was on duty at the Cross nearby and the two went off to have breakfast together. He said that he was feeling bad, with pains in his heart. Devey told him to take some sal volatile. Then Burrows said, 'Have you heard about the affair at the *Garibaldi*?' He said that he had heard that two people were dead, and that they had been shot. He described to Devey how they were found. He added that the kiddie was dead in bed, that the drawers had been pulled out and money

scattered about. Several bottles of whisky were on the table, opened but not emptied.

Ten minutes later he said, 'Funny thing, Billie, I was having two glasses of whisky with "Ern" Laight at twelve o'clock. I was the last with him.' He asked Devey if this would stop him going on leave, because he wanted to go to London. Devey said that he did not think it would. A few minutes later PC Burrows asked the same question again. At this Devey became annoyed. He answered sharply, 'Do you think the police force can't do without you?' It was obvious that all was not well with PC Burrows. Devey reported the conversation to Detective Sergeant Fisher.

Burrows was on a tour of duty from 6 am to 2 pm, after which he was due to go on leave. At one o'clock he was fetched from his beat by Detective Sergeant Fisher. First Fisher asked him at what time he had left the inn the previous evening. Burrows replied 'at about ten-thirty'. Then Fisher asked him how he knew about the murders so quickly; Burrows said that he had been told by a man from Webb's in Lower Moor. He added that he hoped that this would not affect his leave. Fisher told him to remain in the station. Burrows was lodging with Mrs Simpkins at 92 Wyld's Lane, so Fisher collected Detective Constable Beasley and they went to search Burrows's rooms.

They found in his room some £1 notes, ten shilling notes, some silver and a sovereign and a mounted sovereign, amounting in all to about £87. Four tokens for the automatic machine in the *Garibaldi* were scattered about on the floor. In a locked drawer in his bedroom was a revolver with five live cartridges and a box with thirty-five cartridges; three of the cases were empty. Documents revealed that Burrows was heavily in debt to money lenders. Neighbours were questioned: George Sharpe, a clerk living at 116 Wyld's Lane, said that he had seen Burrows in the *Garibaldi* at ten o'clock and he was still there when Sharpe left at eleven-thirty.

At 4.15 pm Burrows said he wished to make a voluntary statement. He was asked whether he wanted to write it down himself, or if he would like the sergeant to assist. He chose the latter and dictated the following:

I, Herbert Burrows, 22 years of age, voluntarily and fully admit to you that I killed at 1.50 on November 27 Mr and Mrs Laight and Bobby Laight. The cause will remain unknown. I apologize to the officers and men of the Worcester City Police for the disgrace this has incurred.

Over the following weeks he repeated the story of the murders many times. First he shot Mr Laight in the cellar. Mrs Laight, on hearing the shot, came down the cellar stairs and asked, 'What is the matter?' Mr Laight, who was then dying, said, 'He shot me.' Burrows shot Mrs Laight when she gave out a scream, and, on entering the child's room to take the cash box, he killed him too in order to stop him making a noise. The constable then returned to his lodgings and had a good night's sleep.

Burrows had only been a probationary officer for six months, coming from New Barnet in Hertfordshire. His father had died and his mother had remarried an ex-police officer four years previously. He was a troubled teenager: at 15 he was bound over to keep the peace and at 16 was found guilty of shop-breaking, put on probation and sent to a boys' home in Carmarthen. From there he apparently joined the navy, where he was not popular among his contemporaries. He loved showing off and liked to be in the limelight. His nickname was 'Duke of Telegrams', as he was always sending telegrams. He boasted to his colleagues how easy it was to wangle leave and often seemed to be absent.

On leaving the navy, he became a chauffeur in Hertfordshire. He then joined the police force and was transferred to the Police Training Centre in Birmingham, where he was thought to be full of promise. The staff described him as a pleasant, agreeable person and a good scholar. His colleagues and his landlady described him as a decent, quiet, kindly man. When he was stationed in Worcester, the *Garibaldi Inn* was his favourite off-duty haunt, and he became friendly with the Laight family. Unfortunately, he had developed a liking for London night-life that required an expenditure far beyond that of his wages as a police constable.

After the arrest Burrows was taken to Gloucester prison, where he was charged on Saturday, 28 November. The first inquest in Worcester was interrupted by police court proceedings and had to be resumed a fortnight later. A huge crowd gathered outside the court to catch a glimpse of him. The train from Gloucester was delayed because of smog, leaving Burrows with only half an hour to spare. There was just time for him to have a few words with his mother through the grill of the cell door in the county police station before he went to court. His mother, described in the press as a 'tall stately woman of distinguished bearing', was so distressed that she was unable to attend court and had to return home. Burrows's brother, Jack, who bore a strong resemblance to him, also arrived. Jack said to the press:

> He was a good lad; he wrote (to) his mother regularly and was genuinely in love with his sweetheart. He was looking forward to his marriage and so far as we know, was quite happy in every way. My mother is heartbroken. She came to Worcester on Thursday to hear the police proceedings but was so overcome that she had to leave for home again. What sorrow we have for him is shared by our feeling of real grief for the Worcester Police and especially the relatives and friends of the Laights.

In court, Burrows stood between two warders, apparently unmoved but pale. There was no doubt of his guilt. The extracted bullets matched those in Burrows's room. Mr Laight's sister identified the mounted sovereign as one she had given the murdered innkeeper. The exact sum of money that should have been in the cash box in the inn was found in his room, together with discs from the automatic machine. His landlady identified the rubber gloves as those she had seen in his room – in the 1920s rubber gloves were a luxury, rarely used.

Burrows's behaviour was unusual, to say the least. While the jury were signing their names to the verdict sheet, he whispered to one of the warders and smiled.

Sensation in Court

The trial was held at the end of January. A rumour had been circulating that there was going to be a new development in the case, and that a counsel had been instructed to defend Burrows. So many people gathered outside court that only a tenth were admitted.

Burrows stood to attention, stiff and erect, and when the

judge asked him how he was going to plead he said 'Not guilty' in a firm, clear voice. A ripple of astonishment went through the courtroom.

During the proceedings he shuffled and shifted, his eyes wandered from side to side as if he was not interested in the affair; but when it came to a report on his medical condition, he leaned forward and took an interest.

His medical sheet showed that while still in the navy, before joining the police force, he had congenital syphilis. He first went into Chatham Naval Hospital with ulcers on his left leg on 18 December 1921, four years before the murder. The disease was diagnosed five weeks later. He was in hospital again in 1923 and discharged from the navy.

Until the discovery of penicillin, syphilis was the scourge of the civilized world, generally known as 'the great pox'. It caused widespread sickness, misery and death. Usually transmitted sexually, the virus can also be passed on to the unborn foetus via its mother, resulting in congenital syphilis. The first phase is a small red pimple which gradually changes and becomes ulcerated. The disease goes through several stages, with periods of apparent inactivity in between.

The virus can attack any tissues of the body. It can produce an inflammatory lesion affecting the nerve cells of the brain, when it is known as general paralysis of the insane; this can occur in congenital syphilis. Among the symptoms are slight loss of memory, inability to concentrate and attacks of depression. If these symptoms are not treated the patient develops delusions of grandeur. He may order expensive items for which he cannot pay and imagine that he is somebody very great.

A test for the disease had been invented by Wasserman in 1906. Accordingly, Burrows was diagnosed, though he could not be cured; Alexander Fleming discovered penicillin in 1928, but the medicine was not refined sufficiently for general use until the 1940s.

Three medical officers were called. Dr Bell of Gloucester prison had Burrows under observation for two months. Mr Fenton was the medical supervisor at the County Mental Hospital in Powick. He talked to Burrows in Gloucester prison and reported that Burrows told him details of the crime with an air of detachment. When Burrows told the medical officer at

Winson Green about the murders, he laughed, as if it were a great joke. All three medical officers agreed that one of the first signs of general paralysis of the insane was great talkativeness and cheerfulness (although many doctors cite depression as one of the first symptoms). It was possible that Burrows did not realize the enormity of the offence as a normal man would have done, though he did know that he had done something wrong.

Burrows said that he was in the habit of carrying a pistol with him and that he had no idea he was going to use it until he was in the cellar with Laight. Then a feeling of helplessness or weakness overcame him, and he used it automatically.

The defence was therefore one of insanity, but when the public prosecutor addressed the jury, he described it as a cold, calculated crime. Burrows had planned it for the end of the month when the maximum takings were in the inn and just before he was due to go on leave. He may have been in the habit of carrying a pistol, but he was not in the habit of carrying a pair of rubber gloves. This proved that the crime was carefully planned and premeditated, not the action of an insane man.

The judge concluded that the prosecution had shown a motive, that of robbery, and Burrows was consequently sentenced to death. The execution took place in Gloucester gaol. However, within a few years he would have been dead anyway from general paralysis of the insane. His limbs would have constantly trembled, he would have been unable to stand, he would have become mentally confused and disorientated and in the final stages he would have been doubly incontinent.

As for little 6-year-old Joan Laight, it was discovered that her father held a registration certificate as a reader of *John Bull* with £1,000 free insurance benefit. This entitled the survivor to £1,000 in the event of the death of husband and wife (permanently residing together) by violence caused by burglars or housebreakers entering for the purpose of robbing. The certificate was not discovered for several days, but it was reported to the authorities within the stipulated time period and a claim was made. The proceeds were enough to provide for the child's education and maintenance, and enabled Joan to live in Worcester with her grandparents. She survived to a ripe old age.

CHAPTER 2

The Gentleman who Murdered his Mother – Upton Snodsbury

The pretty village of Bretforton lies about three miles east of Evesham and enjoys its share of tourists, chiefly to visit the well-known *Fleece* public house, the only pub to be owned by the National Trust. About fifty yards away is the imposing Bretforton Hall, opposite which is a large cottage.

In the early 1700s the cottage on this site was occupied by Mrs Ann Cormel, a gentle elderly lady, much loved in the village. She was always ready to help anyone in difficulties; for example, her next-door neighbour found himself in a spot of bother financially and asked if she could lend him twenty shillings for a short time. Although she herself was not wealthy, she readily agreed. To cover this loan, he gave her a silver box, two rings and two silver clasps. When he came to repay the money, Mrs Cormel told him she didn't want it back, he could keep it. In return for her kindness, he told her to keep the artefacts. Little did they know how significant these items were to become.

On 5 February 1707 the house burned down, with Mrs Cormel inside. Her next-door neighbour helped to dig out her body from the ruins and noticed that her skull had a hole in it large enough to take a clenched fist. It was assumed that a beam from the roof had fallen on her head. The fire was the talk of the village for weeks. How had it happened? Had she taken a candle to bed? Had she not dampened the ashes of her fire each evening?

No one guessed the real cause.

To Live like a King

This is a tragic story not only of a country gentleman, John Palmer, but also of Giles Hunt, a country yokel at the other end of the social scale, a young married man who unwittingly drifted into bad company and found himself at the centre of a terrible chain of events. Hunt was an itinerant farm worker and labourer, and in the autumn of 1706 he became a hired servant to a family in Bretforton. His employer was later to say that he was a laborious, diligent man who did his work well. During the haymaking season, when nearly everyone in the village was required to turn out and lend a hand, he met John Allen, a meek-looking, quietly spoken man, full of misquoted religious phrases. Hunt and Allen happened to bump into each other at the local pub a couple of times long after the haymaking had finished. One evening, Allen brought along his great friend, Tom Dun, who was obviously quite well-to-do but who drank heavily and swore volubly. He had the embarrassing habit of making loud remarks full of sexual innuendos whenever a lady was within earshot.

One evening, Dun and Hunt found themselves alone, and Dun began asking Hunt personal questions, such as, was he married, how many friends did he have, and so on. Then he said that if Hunt came to work for him, he would live like a king and never have to worry about money again. Dun said that it was no crime to steal a purse from someone who could spare it, and Hunt agreed. The latter was under a year's contract which still had a month to run, but he agreed to work for Dun when it had expired. His first job was for Dun's friend and distant relative Thomas Symonds.

The Symonds (or Symmonds) were one of the most respected families in Worcestershire. They crop up time and time again during the history of the county. As far back as the 1450s, a certain Thomas Symonds was Master of an ancient hospital, St Oswald's. By the time of the Civil War, the Symonds family had a grand Elizabethan residence in the parish of White Ladies and it was probably there that Cromwell was entertained in 1651, the evening before the Battle of Worcester. As we will see in Chapter 11, George Symmonds was one of two justices in Worcester in 1661 and he ordered twenty-two Quakers and fourteen Anabaptists to be released from Worcestershire gaol. His son became Sheriff of Worcestershire; the disreputable Thomas Symonds was the son of the sheriff.

Thomas Symonds lived with his wife in Upton Snodsbury, a small and well-kept rural village about four and a half miles east of Worcester. Despite having a father who was Sheriff of Worcestershire, and a grandfather who was a friend of Oliver Cromwell, Symonds was inarticulate, aggressive, surly and bad-tempered. His few words were usually accompanied by a wide range of blasphemies. He spent his days in gambling, drinking and debauchery.

Hunt was given the task of selling a black horse for Symonds for £9 and was given £2 for his expenses. Hunt suspected that the horse had been stolen. He took it to Baseley fair, failed to sell it and was on the way home when he met a carrier who agreed to a swap. When the carrier asked for proof of purchase, Hunt made a hasty getaway, leaving the horse behind. Symonds was not pleased, but Hunt explained that the carrier guessed the horse was stolen. He was subsequently accepted into Symonds's little circle, which included Tom Dun and John Allen.

A Dastardly Plot

At Pershore fair, Tom Dun met Hunt in the churchyard and asked if he would join in a robbery at a house in Upton Snodsbury, where two women lived alone. The plan was that two gentlemen would meet them at Churchill oak and assist them; one of them was the son of the householder, who therefore knew the property well; and Symonds, whose house was almost opposite, was the son-in-law of the householder. The oak was about a mile from Spetchley on the road to Upton Snodsbury.

The house they had in mind was that of Mrs Alice Palmer, the widow of a small landowner. There are now three black and white cottages on the site of her house, known as Bull Cottages. Coming from Worcester they are on the same side as *Bant's* pub but a little further away from Worcester. Mrs Palmer lived with one servant on a modest £35 per year. Although her son had a substantial income, he was continually pestering his mother for more money. He had already borrowed £100, on which he paid no interest, and whenever she asked for its return he flew into a rage.

A row of cottages now stands on the site of the burned house at Upton Snodsbury.

On two occasions Hunt, Tom Dun and Symonds waited, but John Palmer did not turn up. Then, on the third time, on 7 November 1707, he arrived at the oak, a thin, pale-faced man with a brown periwig and hair of the same colour. Later, his neighbours were to speak highly of him and, when in prison, his gaoler said that he was a quiet, sober man, a gentleman both in bearing and speech. He was devoted to his wife, who seemed to be a bad influence upon him, and when the pair were together they were interested only in food and sex.

Symonds and John Palmer were great friends. They were also related: Mrs Symonds was Palmer's mother-in-law. Palmer was rich, his estate brought in an income of £200 a year and, in addition, he had other monies due to him which brought in a total of £740, a small fortune. Yet he managed to dispose of it so freely that he was always having financial problems. At the time of his death he wrote to his executor and told him that he had 'not £5 in the world'.

There are many tales of country gentlemen getting into debt in the 1700s, then attempting to restore the family fortunes by a life of crime such as highway robbery. These debts were often caused by gambling, which had almost become a way of life. Many an estate passed from one family to another because of heavy betting, such as Wick, outside Pershore, which probably passed from the Hazlewoods to the Hudsons for this reason. Landowners sometimes gambled on leasing property for a certain number of lives. The lessee could choose, say, three people and the estate was his for as long as one of those three were still living.

Although Hunt had been working for Symonds and Tom Dun for nine months, this was the first time Palmer and Hunt had met. Palmer asked who he was. Dun said that he was true as steel and to be trusted. Palmer made Hunt kneel down, and said that if ever he disclosed the matter they were going upon the Devil might tear him limb from limb and that the next bite he should eat might lead to his damnation.

When they came to Mrs Palmer's, Palmer stopped, stared at the house in the moonlight and said there was no need to go on. Symonds swore, and said that if he was not to go, nobody would. He reminded Palmer that he had put the matter off twice already. Palmer said, 'Damn her, I never loved her.' Dun asked, 'Is there a dog?' Palmer replied, 'No, there was a bitch but she's safe enough now in Bow Wood.'

Just after midnight, Palmer set himself at the street door and Hunt went over the hedge to the back door. Hunt looked through the window and saw Mrs Palmer sitting by the fire and the maid warming her bed. For some reason unknown, perhaps to fetch in a black kettle standing outside, Mrs Palmer came out of the back door. Dun and Symonds rushed at her: Dun knocked her down with the butt end of his pistol, at which she gave a loud shriek. As she lay on the ground he hit her again and again until the butt of the pistol broke. When the maid came running out Symonds hit her with his fist, knocked her down over her mistress and Dun despatched them both with his dagger.

Dun went to the street door and let in Palmer. His mother was lying face down with the maid on top of her. He pushed his hand under her body, feeling for the keys in her apron pocket. His sleeve was covered in blood. There was a letter with the keys which he read out aloud:

Dear Aunt, I desire to know whether you have received the sweat-oil and the Gully pots with anchovies and pickles that I sent you.

Palmer went to a trunk at the foot of the bed and, unlocking it, took out a box and two sealed letters. Symonds took out a bag of money, about £40. He passed it to Dun who emptied the money into his wallet. They looked round the house for candles but could only find one inch of one candle to light. Palmer went upstairs with the candle and ordered Dun and Hunt to take the bodies up, lie them on the bed and cover them with white linen. Hunt's clothes became saturated with blood. Palmer told Hunt to take anything he wanted; so he took three pairs of sheets, ten napkins, eighteen plates and six pewter spoons, and put them in a sack.

Dun tried to set the house on fire. He put the candle in the folds of the blanket and threw some linen over it, but it refused to catch. So Symonds took the candle and went into the place where Mrs Palmer kept her drink and came out without it, probably having thrown it into the thatch. They were back in Worcester by 6 am and arranged to meet again at Bewdley fair.

Screams and Conflagrations

Mrs Palmer's neighbour, a widow, was lying in bed when she heard a woman scream twice. She jumped up and looked out of the window. Then she saw flames breaking out of the house. She shouted to her neighbours.

They rushed to the house and one of them forced his way in and raced upstairs where he found two adults lying on the bed, each covered in a white cloth. He took up the nearest person in his arms and tried to carry her out but she was too heavy and halfway down the stairs he dropped her. Another neighbour managed to pick her up and carry her out. At that point the roof fell in and they were unable to bring out the second person. When they laid the first victim on the ground outside, they discovered that she was already dead. Her body was covered in blood and there were stab wounds to her skull, face and breast. The maid's body was so badly burned it was impossible to tell if she had died from her wounds.

Libbery, the village where John Palmer lived; even though there are only a few houses in the village today, no one knows exactly which house he occupied.

Mr Palmer's house was at Libbery, a few houses about half a mile away. At two o'clock in the morning he was told about the disaster. He feigned surprise and rode over to Upton. The body was taken to his house. He felt in her pockets and found several farthings that he threw on the ground for boys to scramble for. His maid washed the sleeve of his coat – he told her that he had had a nose-bleed.

On the day of the funeral, every time Palmer's fellow-conspirator, Symonds, went near the body his nose began to bleed. He left the funeral for a while and the bleeding stopped, but when he returned the bleeding started again.

Wagging Tongues

Tongues wagged and neighbours were suspicious. Only a few days previously, Mrs Palmer had said to a neighbour that she feared her son would murder her. A maid remembered Mrs Palmer saying that she knew he hated her and would murder her if he were not in fear of being hanged. On the Sunday before the murder Mrs Palmer had complained to a neighbour that her son had taken away her bitch that was her only bodyguard and used to bark when anybody came near the house. She told another visitor that she had 'lost' her key and had to have a bolt made.

Later, one ex-servant said that her mistress often complained bitterly, and with tears, of her son's unkindness to her, and although she loved him dearly, he rarely came to visit. Another ex-servant said that when the son and Mrs Palmer parted three or four years previously, he dealt very cruelly with her and would not let her have so much as a bed to lie on.

Neighbours noticed that Palmer made no effort to track down the murderer. He did not even send for the Justices until Sunday. He wrote out an advert for the local gazette appealing for information about the murder, but kept it in his pocket. A young man named Francis Hale, who had been pressed into becoming a soldier and had deserted, was hanging round the area. Palmer offered him money to say that he had performed the murder; then promised to help him disappear.

Palmer began to suffer with a bad conscience. He became restless, sometimes travelling long distances so that he was away at night. When he went to bed he paid four people to watch over him, two in his bedroom, and two below.

The breakthrough came two weeks later when a local man told the vicar of Upton Snodsbury that he had seen Giles Hunt going into the house of his brother and his wife early on the morning of 8 November and that he had blood on both sleeves and his trousers. The vicar passed the information to the Worcester magistrate, and Hunt was arrested. He said he had had a quarrel with a soldier resulting in a fight, and that on the night of the murder he had stayed with his aunt and grandmother in Henwick Hill. The two relatives were duly questioned. One said that he had left between two and three, the other that he had left between five and six. Hunt was committed to Worcester prison.

A warrant was issued to search Hunt's brother's house. There they found sheets, napkins and pewter plates, all marked AP. Hunt confessed, stating that he and three others had murdered the woman. He said that one of the men was called Tom Dun, but refused to reveal the names of the other two, saying that he was placed under a curse. However, he gave hints that they were well connected to Mrs Palmer's house.

A soldier by the name of Hawkswood happened to be in the prison and overheard Hunt's confession. He decided to ride over to Palmer's house in Libbery late that evening and tell him about it, perhaps hoping for a reward. Hawkswood said to Palmer that 'if he would come to Worcester he would see some of his mother's goods'. Palmer asked, 'Is it come out? How and by what means discovered?' Palmer said that he would not go straight away but leave it until the next day. He asked if a woman had been accused. Hawkswood replied, 'No, only four men.'

Living with Palmer and his wife in the house at that time was his wife's mother and an elderly relative. Palmer and his wife were very concerned, but his mother-in-law could not understand what the fuss was about. She said, 'He has brought us good news, let us be merry.' Hawkswood saw that his news was not welcome and left.

Hunt's wife and brother came to see Hunt in prison and went down on their knees, begging him to tell the whole story. They knew he was not capable of committing the actual murders. It was late at night by the time he gave the names: Tom Dun, Thomas Symonds and John Palmer. A warrant was immediately issued for Palmer's arrest. Late that night, when Palmer was in bed, a constable arrived, hauled him out of bed, arrested him and made him hand over his sword and a brace of pistols.

The Justices adjourned to the *Talbot* in Sidbury. When Palmer was brought in, Hunt cried 'Guilty, guilty, that's the man.' Hunt was asked what clothes Palmer had been wearing. Hunt said, 'the same, with the same wig'. Palmer said that he had an alibi for the night of the murder. He had not been well and had not been out all day; he had taken physic and was in bed by 5 pm. Because he was not well, his wife had slept in another room. Palmer said that his elderly relative would vouchsafe that he was at home; but the relative evidently decided not to get involved, saying he was unable to remember.

Three constables set off on horseback to arrest Symonds. Since he was not at home they stopped twice to ask local folk if they knew of his whereabouts. Apparently he had hired a horse and left the county. Almost on the point of giving up, the constables decided to take a look in Symonds's favourite drinking place, the *Piddle Inn*. They heard voices in an inner room, opened the door and there he was. He denied all knowledge of the murder and called for more ale, drinking it as quickly as he could. The landlord, John Crump, said that Symonds had given him five shillings for the hire of a horse which was waiting for him in the yard. The horse came in useful, if not quite for the purpose for which it was originally intended – Symonds was sat upon it and taken to Worcester. There was an exciting moment when Symonds reached out and nearly managed to grab the gun of the leading constable, but the other two constables were behind and pushed him away.

Bishop Talbot, who was Bishop of Oxford and Dean of Worcester, was a friend of the Symonds family. When he heard the news he rode to Worcester for four hours through the pouring rain. The heavy floods nearly swept away his horse.

Tom Dun was now to be arrested. No one in the area answered to that name. Several people were brought before Hunt but none of them was Tom Dun. Then Hunt remembered that Dun was sometimes referred to as Hobbins. A branch of the Symonds family with that surname resided at Burford, in Oxfordshire. A message was sent to the Oxford Justices and a description was circulated. Hobbins and his wife were both in church, taking the sacrament, when someone noticed his resemblance to the wanted man. When he came out of church, the constabulary were waiting for him. He was sent to Oxford, then Worcester gaol.

Tom Dun was evidently a Jekyll and Hyde character. As Tom Dun, he gambled, swore, drank and meddled with crime. Under his real name of Hobbins, he appears to have been a model father and citizen and even attended church.

Hawkswood, the soldier who broke the news to Palmer about Hunt's arrest, now played a significant part in the course of events. One evening, soon after the murder, Hawkswood was in a pub with a friend from Bretforton, discussing the events at Upton Snodsbury. The friend happened to mention that something similar had happened at Bretforton. There had been the curious fact that after the fire, a woman had seen a silver box in Hunt's possession containing a pair of silver clasps and two gold rings which should have gone up in flames. Hawkswood and his friend obtained a warrant and searched the house at Henwick Hill where Hunt's grandmother and aunt lived. The box was found. That evening Hawkswood and his friend went to see Symonds and Palmer in prison. Hawkswood told them that they had found the box; Palmer told him to keep quiet about it.

The neighbour from Bretforton was brought and identified the jewellery as Mrs Cormel's. Hunt was now implicated in the Bretforton murder as well. That evening, Hunt was questioned, and when he was shown the box began to confess to the Bretforton murder. However, as it was late in the evening it was suggested that he should tell his story the next morning, and a clergyman was found to record the sorry tale.

Hunt said that the arson and murder had been committed by Tom Dun, Symonds and a certain man named Allen who lived just four miles from Bretforton. The following is his version of events:

On 4 February 1706, a bright moonlit night, the four had set out, planning a couple of robberies at Piddle but the person who knew the property failed to turn up so instead they decided to rob poor Ann Cormel. One of them had remarked that she was poor and didn't have much money but Symonds said that if it was only £5 it was worth having.

While Symonds kept watch in the street, Allen and Dun went to the barn next door and broke though the wall. The two men were about half an hour in the house and when they came out they said, 'We have done her business for her.' They brought out all the money they could find, the silver box and two papers with debts that they tore up and threw away. They showed them to Hunt but he could not read. Symonds felt the heat from the flames. He turned and asked, 'What, have you fired the house?'

They went to an alehouse and agreed to meet at their favourite rendezvous, *Piddle's*, the next Saturday to share the money. Hunt arrived home at 5 am. Each received £22 but Hunt was only given £7 plus the silver box containing two rings and two silver clasps. He could not resist showing them to one of the servants.

Bribery and Corruption

A warrant was issued for John Allen's arrest. At one or two o'clock in the morning, on 7 December, John Bird and his officers arrived at his house in Ashton-Underhill and asked for the master. Allen came down in waistcoat, trousers and shoes. He opened the back door and tried to push past the little group but he was stopped and Bird asked him where he was going. He replied 'To make water' (this was the age of outside lavatories). John Bird replied, 'Don't stir from the house.' With that, Allen attempted to force his way past until Bird threatened to shoot him. Then he ran back through the house, unbolted another door and tried to escape that way.

The four were kept in Worcester prison, Palmer and Symonds on an upper floor and Allen and Dun (Hobbins) on a lower. Palmer and Symonds refused to see any clergymen, but one evening the local vicar was determined to see Palmer no matter how long he had to wait. While the vicar was waiting, a young lady arrived to see the prisoner. Symonds came into the room, embraced the young lady, took her to a bed in that same room and drew the curtains. She stayed with him until he went to sleep. By that time, a number of people were waiting to see them both. Palmer came into the room, woke up Symonds and told him to see the vicar. Symonds refused. There was an argument and Palmer shouted, 'By God, you shall!'

It was time for bribes. The gaoler was given a large sum to allow the prisoners to walk about freely without fetters. An attorney offered Hunt a small fortune to retract his statements. A proposal was sent to the sheriff asking if, for an undisclosed amount, two of Palmer's friends could be on the jury. A message was sent to the sheriff with five guineas (£5 and 5 shillings) saying that this would be increased if the sheriff would influence the jury in Palmer's favour. The bailiff was also offered some money if he would speak to the jury in Palmer's favour.

Palmer had confessed to the murders, therefore it was generally agreed that nothing could be done except protect the reputation of the family as far as possible. However, it was suggested that if he retracted his confession, 'with monies rightly placed', a pardon might be obtained. It was reckoned that the bribes would cost a total of £85 16s 7d, consisting chiefly of a long list of names of those who would require £5 apiece.

Palmer said that he was so drunk when he made his confession that he did not know what he was saying; but a pardon was not granted, only a three-week reprieve. Bishop Talbot realized that there was no doubt about their guilt and that all four would hang.

The trial was held in March 1708, with Justice Powell presiding. Allen was first at the bar. His master and dame arrived with three boys who all swore he was at home that night. When the boys were questioned, they did not even know what the present month was, and the crime had been committed over twelve months beforehand!

He was followed by Symonds, who behaved very rudely throughout the trial. He challenged all twenty of the jury until the judge called a halt. He kept interrupting and asking questions. He said that he did not know Allen or Dun (Hobbins) and only knew Hunt by sight. The local butcher said that he had seen Symonds and Hunt drinking together at the *Red Lion* in Piddle.

Palmer's wife, mother and several servants arrived to give evidence that Palmer was at home on the night of the murder. The more they tried to help, the more obvious it became that they had been bribed to say their piece. One of the servants said that his master went to bed at eight o'clock (not five) and that he never wore brown clothes (which he was then wearing). It turned out that she had only been in their employ for three weeks.

Palmer's maid had washed blood from the sleeve of his coat. He said he was out hunting that day and had taken up a bloody hare. But, as the judge pointed out, Palmer said earlier that he was ill, had taken 'physick' and had not been out of the house all day.

As for Dun, a series of witnesses were brought in from Oxford who all stated that he was in Oxford at the time of the murder.

Palmer and Symonds declared that Hunt's testimony was 'all lies'. However, Hunt's story was corroborated from an unusual and unexpected source. John Washford was a local 'scribe'. It has been estimated that, in the 1700s, about 70 per cent of the population were illiterate and Washford therefore performed a useful service reading and writing letters for the villagers. He was called to Mrs Palmer's house early in November 1707 to reply to a letter from her niece asking if she had received certain items. The judge pointed out that Hunt was unable to read, therefore his story must be true. He must have been at the site with someone else who read the letter to him.

The jury were only out for one and a half hours before they returned a verdict of 'guilty' against all four men.

Final Requests

The day before they were hung, Allen and Dun asked to see the other two, Palmer and Symonds. Palmer and Symonds were allowed to stand at the top of the stairs while Allen and Dun were taken halfway up the staircase.

Allen and Dun were put in the cart together in the centre of Worcester on 16 April 1708. Thousands gathered to watch the hanging, and the day held a carnival atmosphere, with vendors of gingerbread, gin and oranges, sellers of broadsheets and various sideshows. It was customary for the condemned man to stand on a cart below the cross-beam of the gibbet. One end of the rope would be tied to the gibbet and the other end would be a noose, placed round the victim's neck, then the horses would be given a lash with the whip and off would go the cart. The victim died partly from asphyxia and partly from the arrest of circulation by the compression of the large blood vessels in the neck.

Dun and Allen were hung together. The ropes were put round their necks and the cart began to move forward. Dun caught hold of the rope above his head and shouted, 'O Lord, for God's sake, hold a little.' The cart stopped. He looked at the sheriff and asked if he could say a prayer before he died. He and Allen recited the Lord's Prayer and the Creed together. Their bodies were hung on gibbets near the sites of the murders, Allen's at Bretforton, and Dun's near the ruins of Mrs Palmer's house in Upton Snodsbury.

Because of the three-week reprieve, Symonds and Palmer were not hung until 8 May. At eleven o'clock in the morning, they both came out of the prison with the sheriff and guards on horseback. Their superior status had apparently given them the honour of a specially built apparatus so that they were to be hung by the 'drop' method, which gave a quicker, more efficient death. The two men said their goodbyes, embraced, and each climbed up a ladder on the opposite side of a tree. When they had reached a wooden platform that had been erected they began to complain loudly about the Justices. Symonds went first, standing on the trap door in the platform. The hangman caught hold of the noose at the end of a rope hanging from a tree above them and placed it round Symonds's neck, then the trapdoor was opened. Palmer watched the heavings and convulsions of the hanging body with horror. His nerve failed him and he sobbed and wept. Both bodies were placed on gibbets and hung on the same day and in the same place as Tom Dun, near the burnt-out cottage at Upton Snodsbury.

John Palmer's considerable mobile wealth and property were confiscated, because of the crime, and given to the Lord of the

Now a public house, The Royal Oak, *but once the home of Thomas Symonds.*

Manor, who was then the Bishop of Worcester, Bishop Lloyd. This meant that his children were left penniless. However, Thomas Symonds Senior, Sheriff of Worcester, made application for an allowance to ensure that the children were cared for and declared that he would personally be responsible for the education of the eldest son, contributing out of his own pocket if necessary to have him made a Queen's scholar and bred at the College School.

Bishop Lloyd refused to take the money, describing it as 'the price of blood'. Instead, in 1713, he handed it over to maintain two schools in Worcester; one of them became known as Bishop Lloyd's School.

The road has now changed; at that time there was no main road and a narrow lane led to the house, wound its way round the back of the cottages and crossed Bow Brook. This is where the three gibbets were placed. The footpath is now so overgrown that it has almost disappeared. Symonds's house later became a public house named *The Royal Oak*, but until recently known as the French House; it has now reverted to its original name.

CHAPTER 3

Death to the Vicar! – Oddingley

This is the story of five parishioners who, in 1806, planned to murder the vicar. Not one of them was punished for it, at least, not in this world!

If you owned a piece of land belonging to the church, it was customary to pay a tithe, usually one tenth, of any produce or stock. This was for the maintenance of the clergy and other church purposes. As late as the 1970s, the Redditch Development Corporation discovered that the piece of land it had purchased from Ipsley church was eligible for tithes. The corporation had to pay another lump sum to be released from the obligation. Tithes could be paid in kind, for example, a proportion of any new animals born, a tenth of the hay or corn that was harvested, and so on. Or a sum of money could be

Oddingley church. A dispute between the rector and his parishioners over tithes had been simmering for centuries.

agreed upon to be paid to the church each year in lieu of the tithe.

Oddingley is a small village halfway between the eastern outskirts of Droitwich and Worcester. The amount of tithes that the rector of Oddingley should receive had been under dispute for centuries and the cause of much ill-feeling between the residents and the rector.

In 1793 a new rector was pitched into this long-standing battle about tithes. The living of Oddingley became vacant and the patron, Lord Foley, was required to appoint a new vicar. Lord Foley was anxious to become a Member of Parliament and, as he was leader of the Whig Party in Worcestershire, he wanted someone who supported that party and could find him extra votes. Since Reverend Parker was gaining a reputation for recruiting Whigs up in Cumberland, Lord Foley presented Parker to Oddingley.

Reverend Parker was apparently a frugal man. With only a few servants he lived quietly with his family in the vicarage, and he even looked after his own cows. He was so mean that he asked for a hedge to be cut back, then demanded 10 per cent of the cuttings.

One of the differences between a rector and a vicar is that a rector collects tithes. Reverend Parker was therefore a rector; and as there was no salary for the incumbent of Oddingley, he relied entirely on tithes. The total annual average value of all the tithes was somewhere between £130 and £150. His predecessor had accepted an annual value of £130 in cash, but Reverend Parker wanted more than this. A compromise was reached in that the parishioners would now pay their tithes in kind. This went on for two years, after which the cost of goods increased as a result of the French wars. This meant that the farmers were giving the rector far more than £130 worth of goods. They asked if they could change the terms of their agreement and pay in cash instead, even offering to increase their total payments to £150; but Reverend Parker refused. He also told them that as they were paying tithes in kind, he needed somewhere to keep the animals and store the grain – adding to their burden the building of a new barn and a shed. This was taking things too far: the farmers were up in arms.

The Farmers and the Plot

The leader of the revolt was Captain Samuel Evans of Church Farm, next to the church. Born in about 1733, he was in his seventies at the time of the murder. In the days of his youth he had joined the army, was made sergeant, did very well as a recruiting officer and was sent to the West Indies. Promotion was usually rapid in those days because of the heavy mortality rate, and though the fighting was minimal the climate and the large quantities of rum that were consumed were not conducive to good health. Evans was soon promoted to captain. He eventually retired on half-pay near Tenbury. Lord Foley took a liking to him and made him a Freeman of the Borough of Droitwich. He lived in Oddingley from about 1800 to 1826 and became a bailiff and a magistrate.

Thomas Clewes of Netherwood Farm was also involved; his farm was half a mile south-east of the church, on the road to Crowle. Other landowners heavily implicated were John Barnett, his brother William and George Bankes.

At Easter 1806 there was a meeting in the church vestry between the Reverend Parker and some of the farmers. Parker objected to the amount spent on dinners at their local pub *God Speed the Plough*. After the meeting, the farmers went over to the *Plough* for their customary dinner. One of the farmers

Speed the Plough *was originally named* God Speed the Plough *but were made to drop the 'God' because of a plot hatched within its walls.*

proposed a toast to the health of the vicar. Four of those present, including Captain Evans and the two Barnett brothers, drank it left-handed. That was a signal, 'Death to the Vicar'. A witness later stated in court that a month before the murder she had heard the same group at another meeting drink the toast 'Death to the Bonaparte of Oddingley'.

As eminent members of the community, they could not undertake the dastardly deed themselves, so they hired Richard Heming, probably offering him £50. Heming was born in Bredon. Three years before the murder he had married a young lady from Oddingley called Elizabeth Burton. They had moved to Droitwich where they had three children. His official occupation was carpenter and wheelwright, but he was a shady character and under suspicion for a number of robberies. He was later described by the police as being five feet five inches in height, with large features, a high forehead and dark brown hair, bald at the front. He had a black beard round his face (apparently no moustache), a wide mouth, and dark hazel eyes. He usually wore a blue coat with metal buttons that was too long for him.

In late April or early May he started visiting Captain Evans, ostensibly to do odd jobs. The captain had found him a gun and perhaps he was learning how to use it. His wife kept a list of his visits and in May he charged the Captain for 27 days at 2 shillings and sixpence a day.

Although Heming was able to turn his hand to a great many tasks, murder was a new venture. A woman who lived nearby was later to tell the court that Heming had worn a footpath in a field near the vicarage, walking up and down, waiting for the vicar to appear alone so that he could shoot him.

Murder! Murder!

On 24 June 1806, Parker went to bring in the cows. His young daughter usually accompanied him, but on this occasion he was alone. Heming was waiting behind a hedge, the very hedge that the vicar had asked to be cut and for which he had taken the tithes.

It must be said that Heming was very thorough in his task. First of all he fired at Reverend Parker. The rector fell, screaming

'Murder! Murder!' Then Heming ran up to him, saw that he was not dead and beat him with the butt of the gun so violently that he broke it. To make sure the job had been done, he set fire to the injured man. Unfortunately, he took so long over the murder that he was seen.

Two local butchers, Thomas Giles and John Lench, heard the shot and the screaming, and Lench ran to see what was happening. Heming threw a bag into the hedge and started walking towards Lench. There are two different accounts of their conversation. The press reported that Heming put a hand to his hip pocket and shouted 'Come any nearer and I will shoot.' The more reliable reports state that Lench shouted, 'Villain, do you know what you have been doing?' to which Heming replied, 'Me? Nothing,' and ran off. Lench went to see who had been shot and found the dying vicar, 'all of a smoke on the right side'. He started removing Parker's clothes to see where he was injured and found a wound on the right side where the ball had entered. He also had two nasty cuts over his left eye.

Giles ran to the vicarage and told the servant girl what had happened. She sent for the rector of the next parish, Reginald Pynder, who was acting county magistrate. He galloped over on his horse and was quickly on the scene. Parker was not quite dead. He was sitting on the ground supported by several people, but after a few minutes, with a great sigh, he breathed his last. Four villagers carried him back to his home in a chair.

Lench looked along the hedge and found the bag with part of a gun in it. Constables searched Heming's home in Droitwich, but he was not to be found. A parson saw him hurrying towards Worcester sometime between 5 and 6 o'clock that evening. That same day, he was seen at a public house with his coat over his arm. About a week after the murder a girl saw him running into some woods. Heming was never seen in public again.

The inquest was held the day after the murder. It was customary for the borough magistrate to act as foreman of the coroner's jury. This was, of course, Captain Evans. A later investigation discovered that all kinds of evidence had not been brought forward and the whole inquest was rushed through in one day. Captain Evans gave the verdict, 'Wilful murder against some person or persons at present unknown'.

There were so many complaints that the county magistrates held an investigation. Captain Evans was examined on oath. He said that he was so keen to see Heming captured that he was asking for subscriptions to put towards a reward. The county magistrates promptly offered £50 and the honorary secretary gave £100.

Thomas Clewes meanwhile employed a local labourer to cart mud to fill up the floor of an old barn at Netherwood Farm and make it level.

All is Revealed

The years passed. Thomas Clewes found that he could not make farming pay, sold the farm and became a woodman. The two brothers, John and William Barnett, ran their mother's farm.

Captain Evans left Church Farm in 1809 and moved to 'New House' Farm. He lived there until he was 96, dying in 1829. He was a sickly man during those last few years and, three years before he died moved to Droitwich. His maidservant often heard him praying aloud at night, and during the last few weeks of his life he thought the murdered rector came to visit him. He would shout 'Take him away, take him away from my bedside.'

It was thought that Heming had emigrated to America; in fact a letter was received by Heming's wife, said to be from America and describing how he had escaped.

Heming may have had his faults, but he was an affectionate husband and his wife Elizabeth claimed that he would never have gone somewhere without letting her know. She made a great fuss. Three days after the murder a hayrick of clover mysteriously appeared on Captain Evans's farm and stood there, undisturbed. Nearly ten years after the murder, in 1816, it was still untouched. Elizabeth went to the local magistrate and said that she believed her husband's body had been hidden in it. A date was set for the search, but during the previous night the rick mysteriously disappeared. The ground where it had been standing was dug up, but nothing was found.

Heming's three children died. Elizabeth remarried and moved to St Martins, Worcester.

Lord Foley sold the Oddingley estate to Howard Galton, and Netherwood Farm was let to the Waterson family. The farm buildings were in a bad state of repair, particularly one huge old barn. The Watersons asked Mr Galton if they could pull it down. At first he refused, then agreed.

The Watersons looked round Oddingley for someone who could do the work and, as luck would have it, they settled on a 53-year-old labourer, Charles Burton. He happened to be the brother of Elizabeth, Heming's wife and therefore Heming's brother-in-law. Work began on Monday, 21 January 1830, twenty-four years after the murder. Burton started digging round the foundations and found an old shoe with a foot still in it, then another. A little more digging revealed a two-foot carpenter's slide rule. He immediately suspected foul play, covered the hole with stones and notified the police. Heming's wife identified the shoes and rule as belonging to her husband, the shoes by the nails in the heels and the turned up toes, and the rule by a crack in it when it had been dropped. Two days later a surgeon arrived from Worcester to be in charge of the excavations. The soil was loose and easily removed. At a depth of two and a half feet, in a narrow grave, lay the skeleton of a man. He was lying on his left side with his back towards the foundation wall, as if he had been thrown in. The bones of his left arm were under his head and his right arm covered his ribs. His skull was cracked from the forehead to the top of his head and his upper and lower jaws were broken.

He was about five feet three inches in height, and had been buried in his shoes with the rule in a hip pocket. There were remnants of a woollen waistcoat and corduroy trousers. In the surrounding earth was found a whetstone, a clasp pocket knife and various small coins.

Only two of those involved in the crime were still alive, Thomas Clewes and John Barnett. Captain Evans had died the previous year. As Clewes had been living at Netherwood Farm when Heming disappeared, he was arrested.

The inquest was held at the *Talbot Inn*. This time it was thorough and took five days. On the third day there was a sensation. Clewes's gaoler appeared in court and stated that Clewes wanted to make a statement to the jury. The following

The rector is murdered.

is a summary, in which it appears that Captain Evans had enlisted the help of James Taylor, a local farrier, well known for his drunken habits. Clewes stated:

> The morning after the murder, Captain Evans, George Bankes and James Taylor knocked on my door and said, 'We

A second murder takes place!

A rotting corpse is discovered. All three woodcuts are courtesy of the Fir Tree Inn.

have got Heming who shot the parson. He is at Evans's house and we do not know what to do with him.' I said, 'I will not have him here or have anything to do with him.' Bankes said, 'He has been lurking down in the meadows.'

I went up to Oddingley later in the morning and as I was passing Captain Evans's house, the captain called to me and said that he had had Heming at his house that morning. He said, 'He is lurking towards your house now.' The captain had ordered him to get into my buildings each evening and stay there during the day so that neither I nor any of my family would see him. He added that something must be done for him. 'We must give the poor devil some money or something and send him off.'

He said that he would come down to my house that evening and bring somebody with him. He asked me to come to the barn that evening and said it would not take a minute. I refused and said I didn't want to go. The captain said that there was no need to be afraid.

I went into the barn as the clock struck eleven. The captain had brought along James Taylor and George Bankes, who was wearing a smock frock. As soon as I arrived, the captain called out, 'Halloa Heming, where be'est?' Heming called out 'Yes sir.' The captain pulled a lantern from under his coat and called out, 'Get up Heming, I have something for thee.' Heming was lying covered in straw. As he was rising up, Taylor hit him two or three times with a blood stick (a hardwood stick filled with lead, used by farriers to cut horses' veins). I said, 'This is bad work, if I had known I would not have come.' Taylor hit him again until the captain said, 'He has got enough.'

Taylor said, 'What is to be done with him now; we must not take him out of doors, somebody may see us mayhap.' He went and fetched a spade. He searched round the bay, found holes where dogs and rats had scratched, and dug into the soft soil. He said to the captain, 'This will do for him.' The captain and Taylor pulled Heming down, dragged him across the floor, put him in the hole dug for him and Taylor covered him up.

The captain said to Taylor, 'Well done boy. I will give you another glass or two of brandy.'

The whole affair did not last half an hour. I went home and went to bed.

Later, at Pershore fair, Clewes was handed two packets of 'hush' money by Bankes and Barnett, totalling £27.

Despite the captain referring to Taylor as 'boy', it was noted that Taylor was very elderly at the time of the murder and would not have had the strength to inflict the blows as described by Clewes.

At the end of the fifth day, the jury found the following verdict: Thomas Clewes and George Bankes guilty of wilful murder; John Barnett, an accessory to such murder before the fact. The three men were arrested and imprisoned to be tried at the next Assizes. Everyone expected the three men to be sentenced to death.

On the final day of the Assizes, the judge, in his summing-up, said that the Reverend Parker appeared to have been murdered by the hand of Heming, and Heming appeared to have been murdered by James Taylor. Thomas Clewes, George Bankes and John Barnett were accessories to the murder. However, the rule was that an accessory could not be tried until the principal had been convicted of the crime. This could not be done because Heming and Taylor were dead. Until that had been proved,

Thomas Clewes became the licensee of the Fir Tree Inn.

there was not any crime known to the court so there was nothing to which there could be any accessory.

The under-sheriff informed the three men that they were released from custody, and they walked free. When the news spread, the church bells were rung. In the church a party was held with drinking and smoking, though it ended with a fight. The bells were also rung the following day but then the rector, the Reverend Tookey, returned from a few days' absence and put an end to the festivities.

Oddingley church was almost totally rebuilt half a century after the murder, but there are still some parts which would have been known to the Reverend Parker, such as the ancient font, the bench ends and some beautiful late medieval stained glass.

Because of its involvement in the plot, the inn known as *God Speed the Plough* was ordered to drop the word 'God', and is now known simply as *Speed the Plough*.

Thomas Clewes became the landlord of the *Fir Tree Inn* at Dunhampstead, near Oddingley. If you visit the inn you will find a 'Murderer's Bar' where press reports and other information about the murder are hung on the walls.

CHAPTER 4

Murder on the Christian Shores – Stourport-on-Severn

I n 1836, when this murder took place, Stourport-on-Severn was a new town. Seventy years earlier, the brilliant civil engineer James Brindley had arrived to build a navigational link between the River Severn and the Staffordshire and Worcestershire canal. Previously the area had been a sandy waste, known as Lower Mitton. The town developed as a great inland port, with buildings added to satisfy various demands. Industry boomed. The canal and many of the early basins and locks are still in existence.

On the other side of the River Severn stood the small village of Areley Kings, where the environment was more refined. The village was partly separated from the chaos of the town by a flood plain where there was once a ford and an ancient hermitage. High above the river is an old, restored church, where Layamon, the writer and historian, preached in the 1100s.

The bridge between Stourport and Areley Kings, and the road beyond, was subject to tolls. At a public meeting to discuss the abolition of the tolls, a resident pointed out that the houses of Areley Kings were larger and better than those on the other side of the river, and that the folk who lived there may not want all the black sheep of Stourport-on-Severn on their side of the river. Areley Kings was promptly christened 'the Christian shores', and the name stuck.

It was on these 'Christian shores' that one of the nastiest murders in Worcestershire took place. A country road now known as Areley Common runs through the centre of Areley Kings, and along each side is a scattering of shops and stores. On the right-hand side of the road leading from Stourport and about a mile from the town was, in September 1836, a small 'hucksters' shop. The shopkeeper was Joseph Hawkins, a pleasant retired naval gentleman, by profession a navigator, directing the course of boats and vessels. He was 70 years of age, well liked and well respected. As he lived alone, having never married, a local lady looked after him, taking his washing and pressing his clothes so that he always looked smart. Hawkins was a large man, with a stout athletic frame and in good health except for his lungs. He coughed and wheezed and at night he was not able to lie down but slept upright in a comfortable armchair downstairs. Although he had been in the area for thirty years or so, it was only at the end of March that he had moved into the shop premises, where he supported himself by selling inexpensive odds and ends such as bacon, cheese, sugar and tobacco. On Wednesdays and Saturdays he went to Stourport market in order to restock the shop.

The houses along that stretch of road were about twenty yards apart, with huge gardens usually containing a well, a large vegetable patch and a pigsty. Most of the gardens were open, with no fence or ditch dividing one garden from another. Hawkins's house had two rooms downstairs, one of them being the shop, and two bedrooms upstairs. In the yard outside was an old brewery.

The shop of Joseph Hawkins would have been along this stretch of road.

On Wednesday morning, 7 September 1836, William Randall, a local labourer, managed to catch the shopkeeper before he went to Stourport market. Randall bought a roll of tobacco. This was kept on a shelf behind the counter wrapped up in white paper that was torn in several places. Hawkins measured out half a yard.

At seven o'clock early on the morning of the following day, Hawkins's domestic help arrived to collect his washing. Later that morning, a neighbour, Elizabeth Giles, was working out of doors when she noticed him in his garden. Although she lived about 100 yards away, her piece of land adjoined his.

Randall saw Hawkins at about five o'clock that evening, when the shopkeeper had been gathering sheep dung. Later that evening, while in bed, Randall heard the sound of a pistol shot coming from the direction of Hawkins's house. He asked his daughter what time it was and she said it was nine o'clock. He thought nothing of it.

A Shopkeeper Goes Missing

The next morning, Friday, Elizabeth Giles called at the shop at about eleven o'clock to get some coffee and was surprised to find it locked. Whenever Hawkins went out, he took the key with him, and if he was at home he left the key in the shop door. As the key was missing, Elizabeth assumed he had gone out. She looked through the windows and noticed that the doors of the rooms and the cupboards were open, which surprised her as he was a tidy man and usually got up early. When Elizabeth looked through the window of the brewhouse, her view was blocked by a large wheelbarrow propped up inside the window. She went again at four o'clock in the afternoon and the shop was still locked. When she found the shop locked at seven in the evening, she knew that something was wrong, as Hawkins always asked her to feed his pigs if he was away for any length of time.

William Lightband, a carpenter and joiner, lived in the next house along the road with his wife and toddler. His garden adjoined that of the shop. When Elizabeth asked them if they had seen Hawkins, Lightband told her that he had seen him at five o'clock the previous day.

As she was going back to her own house she bumped into the miller of Areley Kings, George Harris. Mr Harris had also been calling at the shop for some salt and was surprised to find it closed. While he was fetching a ladder Elizabeth persuaded her husband and son to come along. They were joined by the carpenter, William Lightband, who was limping, since, he told them, he had dropped a block of wood on his foot. A lantern and candle were procured, and Mr Harris looked through the bedroom windows but still could not see Hawkins. On the kitchen floor were two pairs of shoes. Hawkins had only two pairs, a heavy pair for outside and a soft pair for indoors, and he always changed when he came in. Wherever he was, he had gone without his shoes.

The neighbours were understandably apprehensive about breaking and entering and so they left it at that and went home. They went again the next morning, Saturday, and when there was still no reply, they sent for the local constables PC Hatton and PC Purser. PC Hatton got into the house through a bedroom window.

The bedrooms were empty and tidy, but when he went downstairs to the shop, everything had been thrown about. Cupboards were open and the contents scattered. The counter was a narrow plank resting on two trestles on which stood a pair of scales. The scoop was on the floor and sugar had been scattered across the counter and over the floor.

PC Hatton then went into the brewhouse: there, lying face down on the floor, was the stiff and mangled corpse of poor Joseph Hawkins. He had been beaten so severely about the head that his left eye had been nearly beaten in and his stomach had been ripped open so that the intestines were hanging out. His flannel jacket had round black holes in it, apparently from shot. By the furnace of the brewhouse were four legs of a stool, each one was about four feet long and ten or twelve inches in circumference. One of the legs had blood and clotted hair on it. A coal hammer also had blood on it. Hawkins's hands were scratched as if someone with sharp nails had grabbed them and pulled, and his knees were dirty as if he had been dragged along the floor. A wheelbarrow had been deliberately placed against the window to hide the body from anyone looking in.

Hardly believing what he was seeing, the constable stumbled back to the shop. Mingled with the sugar scattered on the counter were drops of blood, and on the floor with the sugar scoop was a small puddle of blood. It seemed that Hawkins had been killed while weighing sugar, then dragged into the brewhouse.

The Questionable Alibi

Enquiries began immediately. As Lightband's house was the nearest, he was one of the first to be interviewed. His wife said he had been off work on Monday, Tuesday and Wednesday because a log of wood had been dropped on his foot, but he had returned to work on the Thursday. However, when others were questioned, they said that Lightband had not been at work on the Thursday – they had seen him returning home at about eleven o'clock on Thursday morning.

The inquest was held that same Saturday, and neighbours, including Lightband, watched as the surgeon dissected the body. Hawkins had been shot twelve times in the stomach but,

The Tontine, *formerly the* Stourport Inn, *was one of the most prestigious hostelries in Stourport and often served as law court and lock-up.*

amazingly, the actual shot had done very little damage. It had not ruptured any major blood vessels or pierced the intestines. Instead, he had died from the severe beating. His skull had been fractured in several places, the breastbone had been broken and the stomach ruptured to such an extent that his liver had been torn in two.

The inquest then moved to one of Stourport's best hotels, the *Stourport Inn*. Inspector Merrifield had arrived from Kidderminster, and at about two o'clock, hearing that Lightband's alibi had not been verified, he asked for him to be found. This took only a few minutes, as Lightband was already drinking in the taproom of the inn. Since he could not adequately explain why he had been seen returning home when his wife thought he was at work, the inspector detained him at the inn and also called for his wife.

Lightband was searched: his purse contained two sovereigns (a gold coin, then worth £1), half a sovereign, 7 shillings and sixpence and a pawn ticket. On being asked how he came to have so much money he replied, 'I worked for it.'

He also had a silver watch, which he said was borrowed from the local watchmaker, Mr Bickerton, while his own was being repaired. When the police checked with Mr Bickerton, they discovered that Lightband had taken his own watch in to be repaired four months ago, and had gone to collect it the previous day (Friday), though it had still not been repaired. Obviously, Mr Bickerton had heard of Lightband's reputation and guessed that he would not be paid. To Mr Bickerton's surprise, Lightband produced two sovereigns and bought another silver watch.

Lightband had suddenly paid off several long-standing debts. He had owed six months' rent and had called in at the agent's office many times with various excuses, but at nine o'clock on the day after the murder he was in the office with £3, which covered most of the arrears. He also asked a friend of his to take thirty shillings to a shoemaker in Ombersley. The friend was surprised to see him with so much money. A tailor in Astley had made a suit for Lightband but had never received payment, and the suit had never been collected. When, on the Friday, Lightband had called with the money, he found that the tailor had pledged the suit to the pawnbroker, so he received only the pawn ticket. They had a chat about the murder. Lightband went to the Stourport draper, bought a hat and ordered a set of monogrammed handkerchiefs.

Both Lightband and his wife were kept at the inn until midnight. Between eleven and twelve o'clock, their house was searched. In the brewhouse was found a roll of tobacco, a bag of currants and a bag of raisins. Lightband said he didn't know how they got there and that someone must have put them there. It will be remembered that William Randall bought a roll of tobacco wrapped in torn white paper from the shop on the Wednesday. He immediately recognized the roll as that belonging to Hawkins. The labelling on the raisins and currants were later identified by the handwriting on the labels as those supplied to Hawkins.

The inquest was adjourned at Saturday midnight, to be continued at eleven o'clock on the Monday. Inspector Merrifield did not take a day off. Early the next morning (Sunday), he returned to Hawkins's house and resumed the search. In the brewhouse were parts of a gun, but the stock had been forcibly removed by a chisel. A smell lingered about the gun, as if it had been fired recently. Lightband said that there was a barrel, lock and other parts of a gun in the house but no stock, which had been burned a long time ago and consequently the gun could not be used.

However, the miller from Astley came forward. John Overton particularly remembered Lightband, who had collected twelve gallons of flour but never paid for it. Mr Overton said that, as he was going along the turnpike road to Kidderminster market at about eleven o'clock on Thursday morning, he could see into Lightband's garden, and Lightband was standing there with a new gunstock in his hands, ready to fix it to the barrel of a gun. Overton said that he particularly remembered the incident because he was surprised that Lightband, who never had much money, should own a gun. Lightband had not noticed John Overton passing by and as he heard the evidence, he began to choke.

The inquest concluded and the jury retired. Lightband was held in an upper room of the *Stourport Inn*, handcuffed to the constable from Astley. When Inspector Merrifield went upstairs to fetch the prisoner, Lightband said that he wished to confess. As he could neither read nor write, the confession was written down by the inspector. First Lightband described where he had bought the powder, shot and caps, afterwards meeting his friends at a beer shop and spending the rest of his money on a quart of beer. That same evening, he charged the gun. On the Tuesday when he was off work with an injured foot, he walked into Stourport, bought some wood and repaired a fence. When his wife went upstairs, he took the gun out, concealed it in the pigsty and covered it over with a cloth. When his toddler followed him out and pulled the cloth off, he remonstrated with him and covered the gun again.

His account of the murder makes horrific reading. Those of us who have sat by the bedside of the dying know that death is not the quick, clean process favoured by the media. It is too often accompanied by convulsions, twitches, groans, snoring and the death rattle in the throat.

On the Tuesday, I watched my opportunity and about half-past six o'clock I went into Mr Hawkins' shop with the gun, and ordered him to serve me with half-a-pound of cheese, and while he was weighing it I put the gun across the counter, thinking to shoot him, and the cap went off, and it missed fire; he considered me only in a joke and laughed at me. On the Wednesday morning I went to work, and returned home at night. I really had hurt my foot. On the Thursday morning my wife asked me if I was going to work. I said 'Yes': she told me I should be too late; I left to go to work, she left to go hop-picking. I had concealed myself and returned; I got into the house, and set to work at the gunstock and very nearly finished it; draw'd the charge that was in and put it all together and re-loaded the gun with about two thimbles-full of shot. About a quarter past five o'clock in the same evening, I saw Randall speaking to Hawkins; he asked Randall what o'clock it was? He told him it was very near half-past five o'clock; between that time and six o'clock he was dead, and I was at Stourport. I mean Joseph Hawkins. I went in and asked him for half-a-pound of sugar, and while doing so, I shot him the same way I tried before: he fell; I afterwards struck him with the stock of the gun, on the head, when the stock broke; I afterwards dragged him to the back room, and he made a little noise, I found a coal-hammer and struck him twice on the breast, I was then going to leave him and he began to groan; I took hold of the leg of a stool that has been produced today and with that struck him on the same place that I had struck him with the gun stock; I laid hold of him and turned him over, and then left him. I went into the shop; I took about 2*s* 6*d* in copper, and some silver, in all, copper and silver, 20*s* 10*d*. I fastened the doors with the key and came out. On Friday morning I went in again, about a quarter past six, and found him dead; I then went upstairs, and opened his box, and found nothing there; but in an old basket in the room, in removing some old rags, I found five sovereigns and a five-pound note. The things that were produced by William Merrifield were taken by me from the shop. I mean the currants, plums, sugar and tobacco. I declare in the presence of God, that what is here is all true, and I am the only person concerned. The gun stock I burnt.

The jury, without retiring, returned a verdict of wilful murder against Thomas Lightband. As he was unable to sign his name, he made his mark with a cross. He was told that he was to spend the night in Kidderminster, to be transferred the next day to the county gaol in Castle Street, Worcester. He begged to see his wife, but his request was refused, and that was the only time he showed any emotion. He broke down and collapsed. For a few minutes, his gaolers thought he was going to deprive them of the pleasure of seeing him hanged.

The general consensus of opinion was that William Lightband did not look like a murderer. He was 28 years old, a quiet, decent, respectable-looking man with rosy cheeks and red whiskers. He was born in Dudley and came from a large family. He had been bound as an apprentice to a Mr Nuttall, a wheelwright and sawyer in Bromsgrove, but ran away before the apprenticeship was finished. For some time he lived at Ombersley and had moved to Areley Kings only about nine months previously. His wife was the same age and a sweet, pretty woman, who had been in service to a local vicar before she married. She had one child and was expecting another – in fact the child arrived while her husband was in prison. She said later that he was a tender and loving husband.

Lightband sees the Light

Lightband stated that he was going to live to the full the last few months of his life, no doubt intending to spend most of it in a drunken stupor. However, the local clergy had other ideas. Here was a soul that needed to be saved by Grace and rescued from the fires of hell. To this end, it was advisable that he should be able to study the Bible, and they therefore set about teaching him to read and write. The murder had been so bungled that they expected to be dealing with someone of low intelligence, but, to their surprise, he turned out to be very bright. He was quick to comprehend and had a retentive memory. By the time of his death he could read the Bible fluently.

The Reverend Wharton spent a lot of time with him. He asked the prisoner why he had not simply robbed the shopkeeper instead of killing him. Lightband said that he had been planning the murder for some days and had even dreamed about it. He also said that, with his carpentry skills, he could earn thirty shillings a week, a good sum in those days, but he had fallen in with the wrong company and spent his days drinking and idling in the local pubs.

The Lent Assizes were held on Monday, 6 March 1837. Lightband pleaded 'not guilty'. Did he really believe he could get away with it after all the evidence piled up against him? The outcome was obvious. At the end of the trial the judge put on his black cap and said that the awful moment had arrived when Lightband was to receive the sentence for his offence that was so amply deserved. He continued, 'In the whole course of my experience I have not heard of so determined and brutal a murder.' While the judge was summing up, Lightband stood with his back to the jury, his head bowed, tears streaming down his cheeks.

He was due to be executed on Thursday, 23 March. On the previous Monday, his wife and mother were with him for two hours. When the time came for them to part, they clung to each other and sobbed. Over the next three nights, Lightband had very little sleep.

When he woke up early on Thursday morning the world had turned white under a heavy fall of snow. First he was visited by the chaplain, then he managed to eat a good breakfast. At a quarter past eleven, all the prisoners were assembled in the chapel. Lightband entered, flanked by two warders, for a long service. After the prisoners had left the chapel, the under-sheriff formally demanded the prisoner's body after his death.

Lightband was taken to the gallows in front of the county gaol. Many of the roads were blocked because of the snow and so the crowd watching the execution was much smaller than usual. Sometimes a hanging was celebrated with a party atmosphere, but this time the crowd was quiet and watched silently. As Lightband went to his place of execution, his nerve gave out and he sobbed. The cap was put on his head and his arms were pinioned. He thanked those who had been so kind to him during his last few months in prison, then the cord was put round his neck. As he climbed up the steps to the scaffold

The murdered shopkeeper, Joseph Hawkins, was laid to rest in this picturesque spot.

he said, 'The Lord have mercy on my soul.' The chaplain began reading the burial service and when he came to the words 'In the midst of Life we are in Death', the bolt to the trapdoor was drawn.

When it became clear that Lightband was dead, he was cut down and taken into the prison. Several scientists, presumably phrenologists, were keen to get a plaster cast of his head, so his hair was shaved off and the casts made. His body was buried in the grounds of the prison.

His wife went with her two children to her husband's home town of Dudley, where a relative waited to give them a home.

Shopkeeper Joseph Hawkins was buried in the lovely church-yard at Areley Kings, overlooking the Teme valley. There was no money for a tombstone, nor any great crowds at his funeral, only a few of the old inhabitants.

Chapter 5

Death of a Hop-picker – Kidderminster

Two people confessed to the murder featured in this chapter, but neither of them was charged. Why do innocent people confess to crimes? Criminologists have asked themselves this question for centuries. In the United States alone, through technological advances such as DNA, up to 157 wrongful convictions have been uncovered. These erroneous arrests came about chiefly because a suspect made a false confession.

Psychologists have put forward a number of theories. Certain mental disorders can drive a person to seek notoriety. Other people have difficulty distinguishing fact from fiction, or there may be a desire to help and protect the real criminal. Occasionally, a person feels guilty over a crime committed in the past and feels an unconscious need to make amends by confessing to another crime.

Although bullying and beating a suspect in police custody is now banned, there are many psychological techniques that can be used to force people to confess, such as telling a suspect that he can go home if he confesses, or saying that he or she will be charged with a more serious offence if a confession is not forthcoming. Other techniques include lengthy interrogations, denying food and water, putting the suspect under bright lights, offering sympathy and understanding as to why the crime was committed, and telling the suspect that others have confessed, when they haven't.

A Ghastly Scene

The opening paragraph of the *Kidderminster Times* of 13 October 1903 is entitled 'A Ghastly scene in a country lane'. It reads:

A terrible crime, the like of which has not been committed in the district within the memory of the present generation was discovered in the early hours of Sunday morning... Naturally enough the news created a profound sensation in the town and immediate district and for some time there were not a few among the inquiries who ... thought the rumour was a hoax, as many years have elapsed since a murder was committed in the locality ...

On the morning of Sunday, 4 October 1903, Fred Perry, a local cowhand, started out from his home at six o'clock, collected a herd of cows and began driving them up the narrow lane, now Cobham Road, leading from the Worcester Road to Aggborough Farm. On the way, the leading cows stopped and would not go on, appearing to be frightened of something. Fred pushed his way through the herd and reached the front. There lay the body of a woman, her head in the hedge and her legs sticking out into the road. He could see that her legs were badly lacerated; fortunately, the weak morning light and the grass of the verge prevented him from seeing the extent of her injuries.

He continued driving his cows down the lane and then, when they were safely installed in the milking shed, he went to tell the farmer, Mr Whitehouse. The farmer's son, Thomas, quickly saddled up his horse and rode over to the Chester Road police station to inform PC Drew. All hell was let loose. Along came Sergeant Drew in charge of the petty sessional division, Sergeant Smith of Kidderminster Borough Police, Inspector Brazier, Deputy Chief Constable Waseley, Superintendent Walker of Stourport, Superintendent Hinde of Stourbridge, and Chief Constable Bennet of the Borough Force. Within the hour all the roads out of Kidderminster were closed and anyone leaving the town had to give an account of themselves, especially any strangers.

Cobham Road now runs through a housing estate, but in 1903 it was a country lane, almost as deep as it was wide. Hawthorn hedges rose fourteen feet on each side and the lane itself was only sixteen feet in width. It was used by very little traffic and was popular with both courting couples and itinerants, such as tramps and hop-pickers, who slept under its hedges.

The bloodied remains of a near-naked woman lay on her back staring up at the sky, her hands above her head. She had been the victim of a frenzied and savage attack. Her bodice was open and her corset unfastened. From the top of her head to her knees she had been repeatedly stabbed and the skin ripped apart. On the face and neck alone were more than two dozen stab wounds, her nose was broken and her eye blackened. Bizarrely, three of the punctures seemed to have been made with a fork, and scratches down her face looked as if a wire had been used. Among them were ten deep punctures on her forehead, as if the murderer had tried to look into her brain. The fatal blow had probably been the large hole under her right ear, which had severed the external jugular vein. A deep cut encircled her chest and the flesh had been cut away from the muscle as if there had been an attempt to scoop out her breast. On the right side of the stomach was a seven-inch cut, revealing her internal abdominal muscles. The backs of both hands were bruised and blackened, and so was her face, as if she had tried to protect herself. There was also heavy bruising to the tops of her thighs and the left leg had almost been cut off.

On top of the body lay a small pocket knife. The blade and the blade socket were covered in blood. A few feet from the body was a fork with a bent handle. These were apparently two of the murder weapons, although the pocket knife was not large enough to inflict some of the wounds.

The body was lying in a pool of blood, though about six feet away was a blood-filled hole in the grass where the woman had bled to death. It was covered over with a black shawl, as if someone had wanted to hide it. Near the pool were signs of a struggle. The road was disturbed on each side, and four feet away was a ridge of earth, kicked up in the struggle. In the earth was a half circular trail, showing where the woman had been dragged from the spot where she was killed to her present position. There was also sign of struggle fifty yards down the lane and the remains of the black crepe bonnet she had been wearing. Where the body was clothed, the flesh was still warm despite having lain in the open during the wet night. The time of death was given at about midnight.

The woman's possessions were scattered around, among them a small knife, a Roman Catholic Bible, some coloured matches and a clay pipe. Most important in terms of evidence were her hop-picker's cards. She had been working for Mr Watkins at Suckley and Mr Depper at Clifton-on-Teme. One card bore the name Mary, with the surname ripped off, the other card was made out to Mary Swinbourne. The police had a name.

The Life and Times of Mary Swinbourne

The body was moved to a stable at Aggborough Farm. Thousands of people visited the scene of the murder, but police put gates at the entrance to the lane. Mr Whitehouse, the farmer, and his son-in-law stood at the gate and charged sightseers a penny to view the site. The proceeds went to the local infirmary.

Because the body was found just off the Worcester Road, the police at first assumed that she came from Worcester. However, some of her underclothing bore the Walsall Union stamp. The police went to the workhouse at Walsall and, to their surprise, discovered that, until recently, she had been an inmate of Walsall workhouse, although she sometimes lived with her son at 17 Mill Street, Walsall. Her husband was still an inmate. Her body was identified by her son and two daughters-in-law.

Mary was 64 years of age when she died. She was short, well-built and respectably dressed in a black dress, black shawl and black crepe bonnet. She had had a hard life, having had thirteen children and suffered the deaths of four of them. Her husband was a locksmith, capable of earning a good wage but he had deserted, leaving her to bring up the family on her own. These were the days before Social Services and Family Income Support. She would have had to take in washing and do any menial task offered in order to keep the family fed and clothed. Her only reward was the workhouse. Her children had nothing but praise for her, explaining that domestic troubles had caused her to sink in the social scale. It was only lately that she had become an alcoholic. The drinking began when she had felt 'dead beat' and discovered she felt much better after two half pints. As to why Mary had been found half-naked in a country lane, her daughter suggested that perhaps she had felt ill and had gone to lie down.

The body was removed to the *Viaduct Inn* for the inquest. Mr Whitehouse, the farmer, was foreman of the jury. It was stated that she was probably alive when she was stabbed, but the other injuries took place after her death. The coroner suggested that the blow to her head or face would have stunned her; then her murderer began stabbing. Perhaps she regained consciousness and clutched at his clothing, which would explain the injuries to her hands. He then held her down by her hands until she bled to death. The cause of death was recorded as exhaustion due to haemorrhage. The jury reached a verdict after only a few minutes' consideration – that she was wilfully murdered by some person or persons unknown.

Mary had been in the workhouse until 15 August, when she announced that she was discharging herself to go hop-picking. She had previously occasionally visited the hop fields of Ledbury in Herefordshire, but had not gone for the past three years.

Occupation: Hop-picker

Around the mid-1500s it was discovered that hops could be used as a preservative in beer-making to prevent the beer from souring. The growing of hops boomed, especially around the Worcester and Pershore areas, and well into Herefordshire.

The hop-picking season ran from about mid-August until the end of September. Until the 1960s, this was done by hand, when thousands of people, mostly women and children, would arrive chiefly from Birmingham, South Wales and the Black Country. Many of the hop-pickers passed through Kidderminster. Although it was hard work with low pay, it meant that city-dwellers had a free holiday in the country. Farmers would send wagons to collect them, and even use specially chartered trains. The latter usually ran on a Sunday and these alone would bring in about 2,000 folk per day.

The hop-pickers slept in barns prepared by moving out the animals, cleaning up the barn (if you were lucky) and putting down fresh straw. The pickers provided their own entertainment, singing as they worked, and enjoyed a sing-song round a bonfire at night. There was a great sense of fun: on the last day, for example, the women would throw any male stranger into the huge 'crib' of hops, cover him with vines and not allow him to go

Hop-pickers in Stourport-on-Severn. (Courtesy Kidderminster library)

free until he had kissed every woman or given her the money for a beer. Many poor folk looked forward to hop-picking as their annual holiday.

While Mary was in the Ledbury area, she wrote regularly to her friends and family. She owed her son-in-law two shillings and a week before she died sent him the money in stamps with a small box of hops. She said that the hop-picking had finished and God knows what she was going to do now. She also wrote to her daughter and sent her some money.

Her last work was on Friday, 2 October in a hopyard at Clifton-on-Teme, where she earned 10 pence. There, a young man had a knife and fork that he didn't want because the handle of the fork was broken, so he gave them to her. She left the hopyard between ten and eleven on the Saturday morning. The owner took a party of hop-pickers back to the *Rising Sun*, in Stourport-on-Severn, where he left her at five-fifteen in the afternoon. He bought her a pint of ale, and when she said she wanted to go to Kidderminster he gave her threepence for the fare. She said she could go in a workman's car for a penny-halfpenny, but he insisted on giving her threepence. She left the hopyards on her own, and she was alone when he left her.

The Wren's Nest. *The busy road from Kidderminster to Stourport-on-Severn runs past its doors.*

She then went on to the *Station Hotel*, also in Stourport-on-Severn.

She was thought to have been seen at the *Wren's Nest Inn* three miles further along the road, where she begged a glass of water. The landlord of the *Wren's Nest* said that she called there about 7 pm on the Saturday. She said she was very tired and asked for a glass of beer. He gave her a drink of water. Afterwards she sat on the seat outside, smoking. She was alone. A boy living near the *Wren's Nest* said a woman asked him to give her some matches on Saturday night, and he gave her some coloured matches. They were found a few yards from the body.

Friends in Walsall were expecting her home on the day that the police arrived with the terrible news.

Rumours and Sightings

Mary may have lived an insignificant life, but in death she was a sensation. Jack the Ripper had terrorized London with five brutal murders in the autumn of 1888, only fifteen years previously, and he was still at large. Rumours spread like wildfire. It was said that anonymous letters had been seen, saying that Kidderminster was next on Jack the Ripper's list. A later rumour said that not only was it to be Kidderminster, but he was to target children. Some children were so terrified that they refused to leave school on their own and mothers had to fetch them. An injured horse was found, said to be from a preliminary visit by Jack the Ripper, though it was finally discovered that the horse had torn itself on some barbed wire. The police stated that all the rumours were fictitious.

A description of the wanted man and a picture of a knife that could have been used in the attack was circulated by the police. Photography was in its infancy and expensive, so the police resorted to a woodcut. The blade was less than two and a half inches long.

Information came in from all directions. Regulars at Stourport said that when she left she was followed by two men who had been loitering about. A man was seen going across the railway bridge in the early hours of Saturday morning from the direction of Hoobrook to Kidderminster. Hoobrook was about half a mile further south along the Worcester Road. A foreign-looking man was prowling around the *Wren's Nest* and tried to induce a married woman to go with him; the woman tried to get a look at his features by the light from a nearby gas lamp, but he hid his face. A lady from Hoobrook said that she had seen someone resembling Mary at the end of Aggborough Lane at about eight o'clock and had spoken to her; she had been alone and went off towards Kidderminster. Travellers told the police how a man had been seen on a Kinver tramcar with his collar and trousers stained with blood on the Saturday night. He had got off at Woollaston and walked into Stourbridge. Another witness stated that a man was seen in the neighbourhood who asked his way to the police station. He said that he had seen a body in the lane while searching for his pocket book and wanted to report it.

A possible breakthrough came from Hoobrook Farm. On Saturday night, a man and a woman knocked at the door of the farmhouse and asked permission to sleep in one of the outhouses. They said they were on their way to Stourbridge. Having been refused, they went on their way. The farmer was taken to see the body and he identified the corpse as that of the woman. However, on Monday the police received a letter from the farmer saying that the couple had returned, so the woman could not have been Mary.

A bundle of bloodstained clothing was found near the railway at Hodge Hill Farm on the main road from Churchill to Kidderminster, about three miles north-east of Kidderminster. Also, a pair of cast-off trousers was found by Kidderminster Corporation. All the clothes were identified and were nothing to do with the murder.

Percy Mallard, a young carpet finisher, was with a young lady near Hoobrook Farm on the Saturday evening. At about eight o'clock he heard a woman cry 'Oh don't Bill' and scream five times. It sounded like an older woman's voice. Percy looked up the lane but just at that moment the moon became overcast by the clouds and everything was in darkness. His girlfriend was terrified. A few minutes later a man passed him. He was about 40 years old and was wearing a light cycling suit and knickerbockers, but he did not come from the direction of the lane.

Charles Sparry, a train driver, was driving his train from Kidderminster to Stourport on the Saturday evening when he saw a man and a woman walking in the direction of Hoobrook. The woman was drunk and the man had his arm round her waist.

There was, living at Hoobrook, a corporation labourer by the name of William Shingler. He had asked to look at Mary's body in the *Viaduct Inn*, and said that he had seen her on Saturday, near Aggborough Lane at a quarter past eight, in the company of a man. The man was about five feet five inches tall, and was wearing a hard hat very low on the crown. He would have been about 55 or 60 years of age, of good average build weighing ten or eleven stone, and he was wearing a dark coat and trousers. He had a moustache which was almost white on his top lip. The woman appeared to be drunk, as she could not walk steadily. Shingler did not take any particular notice of them but as he went past he heard the man say, 'Oh my darling'. The woman made no reply.

On Tuesday a coal-carrier was arrested in a public house in Wolverhampton on suspicion of the murder. He had stayed in a lodging house in Stafford Street on Saturday night and he was unable to give a satisfactory account of his movements.

The police came to the conclusion that he was not the person they were looking for, and so he was released.

On the Wednesday morning the Malvern police arrested a man on suspicion of being involved: his appearance tallied with the description of the wanted man and his face bore signs of having been in a struggle. The man's account of his whereabouts on Saturday night was not satisfactory and he was detained. Later, once it was clear he had been at work, he was released.

A scruffy middle-aged man was arrested in Kinver, probably a hop-picker. He was loitering in the village, begging in the shops and threatening shopkeepers. When he visited the *Royal Exchange Inn* and demanded beer, the landlady gave him beer to shut him up then phoned the police. PC Bowers was on duty. This was a tricky task. The man was an aggressive individual, and if he were the murderer he could easily bring out a knife. So PC Bowers dressed in an old suit, worn-out shoes, slouch hat and muffler. He chatted to the man and offered him work as a hop-picker. They left the inn together and the itinerant soon found himself in the arms of the law. He was later released.

The man wearing bloodstained clothes was identified and interviewed by the local sergeant. He was a soldier who had been in a fight in Worcester and was therefore cleared. There were no more arrests, and interest in the case dwindled.

The Confession

Three months later, on 2 January, George Fisher was arrested in Market Rasen near Lincoln and sentenced to ten days for begging. He was 50 years of age, a small man with a light brown beard, very bald on top but, as if to make up for its loss on top, his hair grew copiously at the back of his head and hung down his neck. He was well known in the tramp wards of the workhouses.

Lincoln prison had a special receiving ward for tramps. A new arrival handed over his possessions, was searched, then given a bath. In addition to the usual odds and ends carried round by tramps, Fisher had some rabbit wires, used for rabbiting, and a little pocket book with red edges, fastened by an elastic band. The warder opened the book, looking for pawn tickets, and placed the book on a table. At that point he was called away. Fisher hastily tore a page out of the book, didn't know what to do with it and crammed it into his mouth. Another prisoner, working in the bathroom as a cleaner, saw Fisher take the page out of his mouth and shove it under the bath. He retrieved it, Fisher noticed and tried to grab it, but the page was passed to the warder. It read:

I murdered Mary Swinford on Saturday evening first in October, at Kidderminster, Worcestershire. God help me. Murder will out some day.

Fisher had spelt the name Swinbourne incorrectly. He admitted that it was his book and his handwriting, adding, 'There's some truth in it, I didn't intend you to have it.' When he was charged with the murder he said, 'Well I will say nothing. I have said too much already. You must prove it.'

The officer in Lincoln prison was writing down a description of Fisher on 6 January when the prisoner burst out crying. The officer asked him what the matter was. He said 'A woman has been murdered in Aggborough Lane near Kidderminster, her name was Mary Swinford, she used to be called Walsall Mary.'

When his sentence for vagrancy was over, he was re-arrested and taken by train from Lincoln to Stourbridge. Fortunately, none of the passengers on the train guessed they were sharing a carriage with a man implicated in a murder. From Lincoln he went to Stourbridge, then on to Kidderminster by cab, then by train again to Worcester gaol. Fisher asked for an almanac as he wanted to know the date of Barnstaple Fair, which turned out to be on 20 September.

Fisher laughed and joked and treated the whole procedure as a game. He chatted to those who tried to identify him, and at his trial he gave a big smile to the people in the gallery and laughed at the superintendent of police as he passed the dock.

A witness swore that Fisher had spent the night in question at Walsall workhouse, under the name of White. The two witnesses who had seen Mary with a man on that fateful night both identified Fisher as the man in question. Another witness in Hartlebury identified Fisher as a man who asked him for hot water at 8.30 on Sunday, 4 October.

When he was shown the knife he said, 'It is my knife but I wouldn't have admitted it if I had known it was found on the body.' He said he had lost it in Ledbury.

Fisher stated that he went to South Molton in Devon on 16 September and stayed there for three weeks and three days, working for a gentleman, Thomas Henry Vicary of Barnstaple Street, South Molton. At first, Vicary was unable to identify Fisher, but, when the judge suggested that Fisher should speak a few words, Vicary immediately recognized his voice. He said that Fisher worked for him from 18 September to 17 October. A wagoner in the employ of Mr Vicary testified that on the day of the murder, Fisher was working with him unloading trucks in the local station.

A young lady, Lydia Taylor, said the prisoner was lodged with her father at South Molton in October. He was well behaved and liked reading – in fact they went shares in penny dreadfuls, popular sensational reading matter covering rapes and murders. On 5 October her father left him to mind the house while they went off to a confetti fete. No blood was ever seen on his clothes.

Fisher had been identified as Mary's companion with his present appearance, a long brown beard and hair hanging down the back of his neck. He now brought as a witness a barber from South Molton, who stated that in October, his appearance was quite different. His hair was trimmed and he was clean-shaven except for a moustache.

Fisher said he could not remember writing the confession in his book. In summing up, his lordship said that if it were a civil case he would have some difficulty asking the jury to come to a conclusion. As it was a criminal case he would need stronger evidence to prove the charges. He suggested that the jury should acquit the prisoner. Fisher had probably sought notoriety and scribbled the note in a moment of madness, as he explained.

When Fisher was released, Mr Vicary took him to a coffee tavern for a good square meal. He suggested that he took Fisher back with him to Devonshire where he would find employment. He said the man was a fool to have written those words in his diary.

This left the case still unsolved. A sequel came to light on 3 February 1914 when a piece of news from Peterborough, Ontario, was picked up and published by the *Daily Chronicle*.

Alfred Kimberley, aged 30, had confessed to complicity in the murder of Mary Swinbourne just over ten years ago. He was being held in Canada as a vagrant. Kimberley at one time lived near Kidderminster. Two Englishmen who happened to be living in Canada, Charles Robinson and Noel Moriarty, went to identify Kimberley at the police station in Canada. They recognized him as a young man they knew in Kidderminster when he was apprenticed to a plumber. They said that on the night of the murder, Kimberley was out all that wet night. He had returned on the Saturday morning, drenched through. Moriarty said that after the murder, Kimberley, who had been 'a good, steady lad, went to the dogs' and left for the States.

Alan Lauder, the organizer of Kidderminster Ghost Walks, adds:

> His confession was viewed as a ruse to obtain a free passage to England, where he would no doubt be able to clear his name.

Was George Fisher guilty? He certainly seems to have been mentally unstable. The police were obviously looking for a dishevelled and bearded itinerant and Fisher at that time was clean-shaven except for a moustache. A man of that approximate age with a moustache was seen by William Shingler on that evening, near Aggborough Lane. Fisher was working at the local railway station. Would he have had time to board a train, spend a night in Kidderminster and return the next morning? Were police looking for the wrong man, or was Alfred Kimberley implicated in some way? Are we to believe the statements made by Robinson and Moriarty that Kimberley's personality changed that night?

This is one murder which, despite two confessions, will remain unsolved.

Chapter 6

Who Put Bella in the Wych-elm? – Hagley

'Who put Bella in the wych-elm?' Over sixty years after the grisly, skeletal remains of a body were found in Hagley Wood, Worcestershire, the question is still being asked.

Today there are still more questions than answers about one of Worcestershire's most notorious murders. There have been countless newspaper and magazine articles about it, not to mention TV and radio programmes, two books and even a play and an opera. And when questions go unanswered, speculation and conspiracy begin to circulate. So, what do we know?

We know that on 18 April 1943 four teenage boys, Bob Farmer, Bob Hart, Fred Payne and Tommy Willetts from the nearby town of Stourbridge were exploring the Clent Hills and nearby Hagley Wood. Their interests inevitably turned to bird nesting – looking for birds' eggs in trees was a popular child's pastime sixty years ago. It was whilst climbing on an old, gnarled wych-elm (in fact a wych-hazel) that Bob Farmer noticed something strange. Reaching into the hollowed-out tree he caught sight of something light in colour. With the aid of a branch he managed to dislodge whatever it was. He soon realized that he had made a dreadful mistake, and what lay on the ground before them was not an egg but a human skull. Shocked and upset by their discovery, not to mention fearing getting into trouble for trespassing in Hagley Wood, the boys agreed to keep their discovery a secret.

It was Tommy Willetts who finally gave in to his conscience. He told his father, who in turn told Chris Lambourne, the police sergeant in Lye. It was decided that the eldest boy, Bob Hart, would show the police where the tree was. The skull was still there, together with a bone sticking out of a hole in the tree.

This was enough to declare the area a crime scene, and police reinforcements were called in from Hagley. Sergeant Skerratt of Clent and PC Pound of Hagley arrived on the scene to make sure that no potential evidence was disturbed until the CID had been called and Professor James Webster, the forensic scientist, had arrived on the scene. This was obviously going to take some time, so volunteers were asked to guard the scene overnight.

The pollarded elm in which Bella's bones were found.

The following day, Professor James Webster, Superintendent Sidney Inight and Deputy Inspector Williams arrived at the wood. The hole in the tree where the remains had been found was too narrow to examine the interior, so a local lumberjack by the name of Jack Pound was called to chop the tree.

Along with the skull were found several human bones, a cheap wedding ring, a bottle, a pair of crepe-soled shoes and

Bella's skull, a grisly find in the wych-elm.

some rotten material. The rest of the skeleton had probably been removed by wild animals. To help track down any vital clues the local Home Guard, Scouts and other volunteers were drafted in to search the wood. Most of the skeleton was eventually found, but one thing seemed strange: the right hand was discovered intact, about thirteen paces from the tree, whereas the other bones seemed randomly spread out. Why this should be was the lead to further macabre speculation.

With the search for human remains over, the job of forensic investigation began under the brilliant Professor Webster. The few skeletal remains were reconstructed to see what could be learnt about the body. It was believed that it was the body of a woman, probably aged about 35. She was five feet tall with mousy brown hair and irregular teeth in the lower jaw. She had also given birth at least once. He estimated that she had been dead between eighteen months and two years. There were no marks of disease or violence on the body. The coroner declared a verdict of murder by asphyxiation.

Now the long hard work began. The police began to check the 3,000 reports of missing women in a 1,000 square mile radius. But to no avail. Publicity about the case prompted a letter from a soldier who said that his girlfriend, Mary Lee, was missing and probably in danger. The police soon found her alive and well. A local medium contacted the police and offered the name and address of the victim after going into a trance by the tree. The police checked the psychic

Dr Webster's brilliant recreation of 'Bella' from the few remnants found.

information out, but drew a blank. An identity card of a woman had been found in the wood, but hopes that this would lead them to uncover the identity of the victim soon failed when the card's owner was found alive and well, if a little puzzled as to how her identity card had ended up in Hagley Wood.

Any hopes of uncovering the woman's identity through her clothing were soon dashed. Surprisingly, there were no labels on any of the clothes found with the body. Perhaps they had been cut out. The shoes that had been found with the body had been manufactured by Silesby's, a company in Northampton. Of the 6,000 pairs that had been sold only six could not be traced.

As time passed, speculation began to grow. The discovery of the severed hand near to the body led the police to contact Dr Margaret Murray, a leading folklorist of the time. She was the author of several books on witchcraft traditions in Europe. She suggested that the severed hand was evidence of ritual activity by a coven of local witches. In the annals of witchcraft and occult practice, it was believed that a severed hand, called a 'Hand of Glory', could detect buried treasure. It was suggested that Hagley Wood/Clent Hills of the 1940s was, as today, used by local practitioners of the occult arts. Some also saw significance in the body being in a wych-elm tree. Weight was added to the witchcraft theory with the discovery of a man's body in 1945 in Lower Quinton, Warwickshire. Charles Walton had been killed with a pitchfork, pinning him to the ground. The village had been rife with whispers about Charles, whom some saw as a 'cunning man', a sort of village wizard. Perhaps, some villagers said, he had been killed by those who feared his occult powers.

It has to be said that the witchcraft theory is no more than speculation, based primarily on hearsay and supposition.

A New Twist

In 1944 the case took a new twist. Graffiti appeared chalked on a wall in Upper Dean Street, Birmingham, asking, 'Who put Bella down the wych-elm – Hagley Wood'. Similar graffiti began to appear around the region. For the police investigation this could be a vital clue as they now had a possible name for the mystery woman. Records were checked and rechecked for names like Isabella, Luebella, Clarabella and so on; but once again the trail went cold.

Another theory that has become popular to explain the mystery involves wartime espionage. In 1941 whilst serving in the Home Guard, Mr Basterfield was called out to investigate a parachute alert in the Clent Hills/Hagley Wood area. Britain's defences were on high alert for German spies parachuting into the country. A thorough search was made of the area, but nothing was found.

Over the years the publicity surrounding the case has brought forward various new testimonies from people who believe they can add something new to the case. One gentleman, Warwick Plant, was a young boy during the Second World War. His parents owned *The Crown* public house in Brierley Hill, near Dudley. He remembers a woman coming into the pub and asking his mother if she could sing and play the piano for money. The woman, who gave her name as Bella, was poor, and Warwick remembers his mother giving her a pair of her old crepe shoes. The two women became friendly, and Bella explained that she used to belong to a concert party in Europe, but with the start of the war she had come to England. And then one day Bella stopped coming to the pub. She was never seen again.

Another letter to the press came from a woman calling herself 'Anna of Claverley'. She urged the authorities not to take their investigations any further, as those involved were beyond the power of earthly justice. She eventually agreed to meet the authorities and revealed that her real name was Una. She had been married to a man named Jack Mossop, with whom she had lived in Kenilworth in Warwickshire. Jack worked in an aircraft factory, not a particularly well-paid job, and they were always short of money. In late 1940 Jack had met a Dutchman by the name of Van Ralt. It was at that time that Jack mysteriously came into some money. He began to buy expensive clothes and even bought an officer's uniform even though he was not in the services. He began to see Van Ralt more frequently and drink heavily. Una could take no more and the couple split. In late 1941 Jack came back to see Una. He was very ill. He looked disturbed and complained of not being able to sleep. He had nightmares about a human skull looking up at him from out of a hollowed-out tree.

Jack eventually confided in Una that he had met Van Ralt at the *Lyttleton Arms* near Hagley. When he arrived, Van Ralt was having an argument with a Dutch woman. Van Ralt told Jack to get into his car and drive the couple to the Clent Hills. During the journey the argument had become more heated, and Van Ralt killed the Dutch woman. Stopping near Hagley Wood, Jack had helped carry her body into the wood where it was hidden in a hollow tree. Una claimed that Jack had died in 1942 in a mental hospital in Stafford.

So, could this be the explanation to one of Worcestershire's most curious murder mysteries? Was Bella a Dutch native who was acting as a German spy? Had she been parachuted into the Hagley area in 1941? Was she the woman who used to sing and play the piano at *The Crown* pub in Brierley Hill? Was she the same Dutch woman who was murdered by Van Ralt?

After the war another informant told a curious story that may just lend support to this theory. Peter Osborne was a British soldier during the war. With the Allied troops' victory in Europe he had been stationed in Germany to help clear up and sort out German files. One file allegedly gave descriptions of several German spies in the Midlands. One of them matched the description of Bella. The file told of a German spy who had been parachuted into the Midlands somewhere between Kidderminster and Birmingham. Her code name was Clara.

In April 2005 another twist to an already strange case was added. A bundle of 1940s papers, found in a deserted Nazi post in Belgium by a British soldier in 1945, were up for auction. Among the papers was a document dated 1940, suggesting that the Third Reich had its eye on the Shropshire towns of Bridgnorth and Ludlow as possible Nazi HQ following a successful invasion of Britain. The documents suggest that Hitler was still hoping to invade Britain in 1941, a year after being defeated in the Battle of Britain.

David Taylor, Chairman of Parasearch, a society founded to investigate reports of ghosts, hauntings and poltergeists, is able to add an interesting twist on the case:

As a young child in the late 1970s I used to accompany my mother to work during the school holidays. She worked at the *Gypsy's Tent* public house (now called the *Badger's Sett*) opposite Hagley Wood. The chefs and bar staff loved to tell me stories about how the pub was haunted. They would tell me of lights being turned on and off, doors opening and closing on their own, objects disappearing, cold spots and shadowy figures being seen. When I enquired as to whom the ghost was I was told it was 'Bella'. For years this story stayed in my mind, but didn't mean much to me. It was only when in the 1980s that a local newspaper reprinted articles about the Hagley Wood body that I put two and two together. Could the pub be haunted by the ghost of Bella?

I wrote a letter about the ghostly reports to a local newspaper, as I had become actively involved in psychical research. In 1999 the journalist Richard Askwith wrote an article about the Bella mystery for the *Independent* newspaper. All the known facts were *neatly summed up – even my ghost story got a mention*! The article was seen by the opera composer Simon Holt, who was immediately hooked by the story, and went on to write and compose an operatic libretto called 'Who put Bella in the wych-elm?' The opera premiered in 2003 to good reviews. It even came to Birmingham for one night in November 2003, when I went to see it. The central theme of the opera has the ghost of Bella appearing to the two boys (depicted as grown up) who found her, and she recounts her grisly death.

That the Bella mystery still exerts a macabre grip upon us is evident. In March 2007, as part of their seventy-fifth anniversary year, Stourbridge Theatre Company staged *Bella in the Wych-Elm* by David Morris. In the same year a book by Joyce Coley entitled *Bella, An Unsolved Murder* was published.

As the years pass our chances of solving the mystery about Bella slowly fade. Perhaps we will never know the truth; perhaps it is better if we didn't.

CHAPTER 7

Calling Inspector Foyle – Lickey End, Near Bromsgrove

944 was a memorable year in English history. Operation Overlord got under way on 6 June, otherwise known as the D-Day landings. Some 6,500 vessels landed over 130,000 Allied forces on five Normandy beaches. English casualties were minor, but on one beach there were some 4,649 American casualties. Cherbourg was liberated by the end of June and Paris followed two months later. In all, 19,000 Americans were killed in the Battle of the Bulge.

Back in the little rural town of Bromsgrove, the local paper was reporting, on average, three deaths a day of sons or fathers on the front line. Everything was in short supply and had to be queued for. The weekly rations hardly kept a pet alive. There were no fashionable clothes, no jewellery, and no make-up, but there was one compensation for the young single woman: the male population had increased by several hundred per cent. Bromsgrove had been selected to tend to battle-scarred soldiers and nurse them back to health. A member of the Health Authority commissioning team who worked on the old hospital sites observed:

At the beginning of the Second World War, hospitals were built on the farmland behind the workhouse, and on the Barnsley Hall site, usually to take men from the forces. Very few people realize how large they were, between them they could accommodate 500 patients.

The first of the hospital sites was behind the old Bromsgrove workhouse, built in 1836. Forty-two years later, in 1878, the workhouse hospital was set up behind it. The land to the rear of the site was part of Norton Farm, the entrance to which is still in Birmingham Road, together with some of the farm buildings. When war broke out, a large complex of temporary hospital huts was erected as a neurological unit for British soldiers suffering from nervous disorders and head injuries on the farmland. In 1943 the Americans arrived and took over the hospital, and the neurosurgical unit was transferred to Barnsley Hall.

The second site was that of Barnsley Hall. The original hall had been demolished in 1850, when the 324-acre site was bought by Bromsgrove Council and a hospital opened there in 1907. Although its proper name was Bromsgrove Lunatic Asylum, it was always known as Barnsley Hall Hospital. At the outbreak of war, three wards were taken over and thirty new wards were erected in the grounds. Barnsley Hall became one of the largest emergency hospitals in the county, taking a variety of casualties including air-raid victims and men from the front. Some patients, especially those who had been disfigured, were encouraged to go into the town in the evening to get used to being stared at.

Trainload after trainload of injured soldiers arrived at Bromsgrove station. One member of the Red Cross who helped to unload them said that he had never seen such terrible sights. There were those who had been severely burned, and those without arms or legs – sometimes without both.

A retired police officer said of the Americans:

They were everywhere in the war. In the evening they used to come down to Bromsgrove in lorries to go to the cinema or the dances. The town was full of them. They were billeted everywhere – for example in Bentley Manor and in Sillins, that's a black and white house between Callow Hill and Elcocks Green. They had a smart uniform and an American accent and plenty of money. The girls loved them. Of course, there were some GI brides, some of the girls were happy but I know a few who came back. They went over there expecting Hollywood and all they got was a tin shack. There were also a few Americans who fathered babies over here. They'd buy the mother expensive presents and the mother would think her daughter was doing really well and turn a blind eye when the couple went off together. As soon as the GI told his sergeant the news, he was shipped out the next day and didn't even have time to say 'goodbye'.

Despite the shortages and the blackout, evening entertainment was plentiful in Bromsgrove. As well as a range of public houses and hotels, there were two cinemas, the Regal and the Plaza (although the latter had closed down in 1944), showing such delights as Cary Grant and Laurel and Hardy. Every Saturday night a dance was held in All Saints' Parish Hall and again once or twice during the week. Other dances were held in halls across the town. Nearly every association had a social committee to organize events. The Home Guard, the Electrical Trades Union, the Red Cross, Bromsgrove Civil Defence Decontamination Services and a range of other organizations booked halls and advertised various happenings. There were fancy dress parties, whist drives, and for those with more aesthetic tastes, choirs and musical concerts. The Americans entered into the spirit and often put on concert parties and variety concerts. Of course, the main aim of these events was to raise funds for the war effort through the two or three shillings charged for admission.

Florrie and the American Officer
One person who was enjoying the arrival of the Americans was 33-year-old Florence Porter. Her family was well known, having lived in the area for many years. In 1944 they were living at the Bromsgrove end of Little Heath Lane, Lickey End. This was a long, winding lane, and only a few yards away and almost opposite the Porters' home was the local school building. Today the village is dissected by Junction 1 of the M42 and other local roads that converge on the junction, but in Florrie's time the village was largely surrounded by farmland. The family was a large one, six girls and two boys. By 1944 two of Flo's sisters were married so that she was the eldest girl at home, and her youngest brother was old enough to join the air force. Her father had been a carpenter but had died a few years previously.

Many families have someone who seems to have outstanding qualities, and in the Porter family Florence was that person.

Flo Porter.

She was an attractive girl, willowy and stately at almost five feet ten inches tall, an unusual height in those days. She had long, dark hair and, despite the clothing shortage, she dressed well. A bright girl, she worked as a clerk in the Time and Wages offices of the Austin Motor Company. Her bubbly personality made her popular with everyone. She loved music and dancing and had at one time played in the local jazz band, but by 1944 she had dedicated most of her spare time to war work and had joined the St John Nursing Division at the Austin works.

On the evening of Thursday, 26 October, Florrie walked into Bromsgrove with one of her sisters, Doris, saying that she had an appointment with a man named 'Hal'. Doris went off to meet a friend and left her in Bromsgrove at about twenty past eight. The previous day Florrie had told another sister, Winifred, that she was meeting Hal.

A barmaid at the *George Hotel* said that between nine and nine-thirty she went into the smoking room to get the empty glasses and saw an American officer with a girl. They appeared to be friendly and were laughing and talking. Later she recognized the young lady as Florrie. She did not see them leave.

Another woman went into the smoking room at twenty to ten and saw Florrie with the American officer. They left ten minutes later.

Their next-door neighbour was an assistant foreman at the Midland Red Garage, Bromsgrove. He was standing on the corner of School Lane and the Birmingham Road at about 10.20 pm when, by the light of the lamp on the opposite side of the road, he noticed Florrie going by with an American officer. They came from the direction of Bromsgrove and turned up

Lickey End School, which has changed very little since Flo knew it.

School Lane, towards Florrie's home. The neighbour was facing north and only saw their back view, but the American appeared to be an officer, wearing a mackintosh blouse with dark trousers and a hat.

That was the last time Florrie was seen alive. About ten-thirty, screams were heard by those living nearby, but as it was a wet and windy night no one took any notice. Florrie did not return home that night. Her mother wasn't worried because she often stopped overnight at a friend's house in Bromsgrove to save the long walk home.

Horror at the School

Rain spread across Bromsgrove overnight and the next morning dawned cold and damp. Two schoolboys were cycling to school, Albert Egan and his younger friend, 7-year-old Louis Price; and as they were cycling in the Alcester Road past the back of the school Albert noticed something blue under a veranda in the playground. He got off his bike and went to have a look. Lying there, on her back, her head turned to the side and with face and hair covered in blood, was the body of Florrie Porter. Her left hand was under the body, her gloves were near her head and

The back of the school from the road, showing the school porch where Flo's body was found.

near her was a large pool of blood. Her coat was open, her skirt was 'disarranged' but her blue underwear was in place and it was this which had caught Albert's eye.

No doubt the sight gave him a nasty shock, but, with remarkable composure, he sent Louis to notify the school caretaker. Telephones were few and far between, so the caretaker went to tell Mrs Smith, nearby, who rang the police. Four police officers were quickly on the scene, joined by the chief constable, the detective superintendent and some American officers. The school was closed for the day and the children sent home.

Florrie's remains were taken to the pathology laboratory in the annexe of the old workhouse at 165A Birmingham Road. Her face was badly bruised on the left eye, the left cheek and the nose. Either she had been punched twice or her attacker was wearing a ring. Evidently she had attempted to scream but a hand had been clamped over her mouth to stop any noise, with more severe bruising. She had fallen backwards against a wall or the playground, as evidenced by the bruises on the back of the head.

She had died from stab wounds to the chest and neck. A stab wound on the left side of her neck had cut the jugular vein and the carotid artery. There were six more stab wounds to her chest, and holes in her woollen jumper showed where the knife had been plunged in. One of the wounds had penetrated her heart and there was blood in the nails of her right hand. Her assailant would not have been bloodstained as there had been no spurting. There was no evidence of sexual activity.

Only one weapon had been used, and as the blade was only just over half an inch wide, the wounds must have been inflicted with great force by a strong person. Since there were no cuts on either hand, she could not have tried to defend herself, which suggested that she was unconscious, presumably from the blow in the face, when she was stabbed. The overnight rain had washed away any footprints or other clues.

An inquest was held the following Monday, then postponed until Monday, 4 December, to allow time for investigations. The Americans were not represented at either inquest.

Bromsgrove Police, Worcester CID and American G-men with military police were all on the case. On Saturday afternoon a large force of regular and special police were detailed to search the Lickey End neighbourhood. Scores of statements were taken over the weekend and there was a conference at the police station lasting well into the night. Interviews were held with American officers and there was an identity parade at the local US hospital. Several American officers from the hospital were questioned.

The police issued an appeal, asking for the officer with Miss Porter to come forward for interview, and a description was issued. He was a first or second lieutenant, aged about 24 to 30, height five feet eight inches to five feet ten inches, well built, low-browed, clean-shaven, bull-necked, dark hair cut close, sticking up and growing well down the forehead. The cut of hair was known as 'a combat crop' in the US army, but the hair was growing sufficiently to be brushed back. They could have added that he was known as 'Hal', perhaps short for Henry (Shakespeare called the young Henry IV 'Prince Hal'), and that he probably wore a ring. Not surprisingly, no one came forward.

All day the following Wednesday, Thursday and Friday, American soldiers were out with 'magnetic' mine detectors, searching the roads round Lickey End for the knife. The detectors were circular and mounted on to long poles. Schoolchildren also joined in the hunt. On Saturday afternoon Florrie's handbag was found lying in some bushes at the front of a house known as Norton Farm. Other articles were found lying nearby. A pool almost opposite was drained and police prodded about in the muddy bottom. Various bits of rubbish were found and several trout were left stranded, but there was no sign of the murder weapon.

Nunc Dimittis

The funeral took place at All Saints' Church on Wednesday. The church was packed. Among the mourners was the superintendent from Florrie's office, representing the directors of the Austin Motor Company. Her colleagues were also present, together with members of the St John Nursing Division. A crowd of sixty women stood outside before the service and were shepherded into the nave by the police. In his address, the vicar remarked, 'The sorrow which has befallen them is of a very extraordinary character, thank God of a very infrequent kind in this parish.' A detachment from the Nursing Division marched behind the hearse to the cemetery. Outside the cemetery gates a hundred or so townsfolk waited quietly to show their compassion. The sisters wept uncontrollably and one of them was so distraught that she was led away from the graveside by some of the members of the St John Nursing Division.

On the Wednesday night, the chief constable stated that the police wanted to interview any driver who had given a lift to an American or British officer or soldier on or near Bromsgrove on 26 or 27 October. Again, no one came forward. The Press were told, 'One of the complications of the case is that the wanted officer may be among the hundreds of US men who have passed on from the local camp to other establishments.'

At the end of the war there was an acute housing shortage, with servicemen returning from the war who had nowhere to live. The hospital was converted into living accommodation, with five bed spaces to each family. Then it became Bromsgrove General Hospital, later rebuilt to become the Princess of Wales

Community Hospital. Barnsley Hall Hospital closed in 1995 and is now a housing estate.

A final word came from Eric Robertson, who, in 2007, wrote an article for Bromsgrove Museum during a project to preserve old memories of the town. He stated:

I can also remember a young girl being murdered in School Lane, they were seen in the *George Hotel*. My mom worked there, and the Police took my mom to all the American bases to identify the man she had been seen with. My mom did find him but because they threatened the family my mom could not say who he was.

CHAPTER 8

The Flitch of Bacon Murder – Foxlydiate, Near Redditch

The Foxlydiate area has changed considerably since the time of the 'flitch of bacon' murder in 1902. New housing estates have spread across its green fields, the winding road between Redditch and Bromsgrove has been superseded by the A448, and the licence of the ancient inn, the *Fox and Goose*, has been transferred to a site across the road and is now the splendid *Foxlydiate Hotel*. On its northern edge was the huge estate of Baron Windsor, created Earl of Plymouth, with one of the finest houses in England, Hewell Grange. Many local people were employed there. Hewell Grange is now HMP Youth Custody Centre and two more prisons have been built in the grounds.

About 150 yards from the Redditch–Bromsgrove Road and on the right-hand side approaching Webheath were two pretty cottages. Most of the property round about belonged to Lord Windsor of Hewell Grange, but these were on the Bentley estate and belonged to the local squire.

One of the cottages was occupied by an elderly lady, Mrs Hassall. She was the widow of a prosperous needle-maker, much liked and popular in the neighbourhood. She furnished her cottage in the best Victorian tradition. White linen with crocheted borders covered the table and the arms and backs of the cottage furniture. Over the years she had acquired valuable pieces of china, and the sideboard and shelves were filled with porcelain ornaments and a matching tea service. Although Mrs Hassall moved with difficulty, the place was spotless.

The cottage was semi-detached, and next door lived the hard-working Annie Middleton, whose son worked as under-keeper on the Windsor estate. Annie worked at a paper-making mill in Beoley for many years, but for the two years before the murder she had been earning her living by cleaning large houses in the neighbourhood. She was 51 years of age, in good health and an enthusiastic gardener, her plot of land was large and she was well known for her vegetables, which she sold to her neighbours. She also kept pigs in a sty at the bottom of the garden.

The villain was her husband, Samuel. He was 46 years of age and gave his occupation as 'hay trusser'. He was a fairly well-built man, with a dark beard and light blue eyes. When he was sober he was a mild, pleasant man but he was subject to bouts of heavy drinking, when he became violent. On many occasions, Annie fled from the house to escape his temper, hiding in the lane or taking refuge in a neighbour's house. One of these neighbours was a sympathetic friend, Mrs Laura Drew, who, eight years previously, had moved into a thatched cottage across the road.

By Friday, 9 May 1902, Samuel had been drinking heavily for two weeks. Evidently, he had run out of money and, knowing his wife had recently sold some potatoes, he wanted to get his hands on the money. Annie was determined that he should not have it.

Loud and violent quarrels ensued. Mrs Drew bravely went into the house to tell him off. The table was upside down and the food, consisting of vegetables and bacon, was all over the floor. Annie waved her arm at Mrs Drew and said, 'Look what my husband has done!' Mrs Drew found Samuel sitting in a chair, apparently quite sober. She begged him to settle down for the night and leave Annie alone. Samuel went to bed at eight o'clock.

Annie then went to Mrs Drew's house and told her, 'If he begins again I shan't stop in the house and I shan't walk the lane all night. I'll come here for shelter – if I'm alive. If anything happens to me, give this to the boy,' (she meant her son) and gave Mrs Drew the £1 18*s* 6*d* she had received for the potatoes. At a quarter past eleven, she went home.

Samuel seems to have had more respect for Mrs Drew than for his wife, as he apparently waited until he saw her house lights go out before he got up again.

Mrs Hassall's bedroom wall was divided from the Middletons' only by a thin partition, and about midnight she was woken by the noise of loud quarrelling. The noise continued for an hour, the voices rising and falling. About one o'clock there were oaths and a scream, the sound of people moving about, then silence. Afterwards she heard heavy men's footsteps going up and down the stairs until she fell asleep.

Conflagration and the Flitch of Bacon

The son had moved out of the home two weeks previously because of his father's temper and was living nearby. About three o'clock that morning, Mr Middleton called on his son and said, 'If you want to see your mother alive, you had better go to the house at once.' The son asked, 'Why, is she as ill as that? What's the matter?' His father said something to the effect that if she wasn't dead by then, she ought to be. He then left his son and went to the house of his mother, and said much the same to her. After that he disappeared.

About the same time Mrs Hassall was roused by the smell of smoke and was terrified to find her own bedroom full of it. The house was on fire! Unable to move quickly, she managed to get out of bed, throw on a few clothes and cross the road to hammer on the door of the Drews. Mr Drew looked out of his bedroom window and saw the two houses in flames. He woke his wife and told her to run to Herbert Chambers (the landlord of the *Fox and Goose*) and tell him to saddle his pony at once and go for Redditch fire brigade, about a mile and a half away. In the meantime, the neighbours worked together to save as many of Mrs Hassall's possessions as possible. They succeeded in bringing out many of her smaller possessions, but the heavier furniture was destroyed.

The fire brigade received the message at four-thirty in the morning and, bearing in mind that the horses had to be caught and saddled up, were at the scene by five o'clock. By this time, the two houses were well ablaze. At six o'clock the roof and floors of the Middletons' cottage fell in, followed by the collapse of Mrs Hassall's roof.

Mrs Hassall was distraught. Her beautiful cottage had gone, together with her furniture and most of her prized possessions. She was too old and poverty-stricken to start putting a house together again.

A drawing of the two cottages after the fire. (Courtesy Alan Foxall)

The fire raged until seven o'clock in the morning. The fire brigade and helpful neighbours then began their search for human remains. A terrible sight awaited them. On the floor of the back kitchen, what was first assumed to be a blackened log turned out to be the remains of a female. They could only assume it was Annie, as it was burned well beyond recognition. The head, arms and legs had burned almost entirely away. Protruding from the body were the ends of the thigh bones, burned white in the fire. The abdominal wall was broken in places by the fire and falling masonry, revealing the internal organs. A dog had run off with one of the limbs and was gnawing at it. This was retrieved and all the remains were collected together ready for an inquest at the *Fox and Goose*. A missing foot was not found until Monday afternoon.

Annie had been lying on her back and beneath her were the remnants of a brown dress and a dark blue bodice, which indicated that she had not changed for bed. Mrs Drew remembered that Annie had been wearing these garments on the day of her death; and in this way the body was identified.

The *Redditch Indicator* of May 17 1902 stated:

> the sickening horror is accentuated when they occur in the quiet seclusion of a country lane, amid the most peaceful and, one would think, the most humanising surroundings, in the very heart of the most charmingly picturesque rural scenery.

The neighbours had no doubt that the fire was started deliberately. It was noticed that all down the length of the garden were trails of straw. Evidently, someone had carried all the dry straw out of the pigsty into the house and piled it up in the back kitchen – the unburned ends of the straw still protruded under the bottom of the door.

Here is a mystery. This murder is known locally as 'the flitch of bacon murder'. The locals will tell you that Samuel laid the body on a bed of straw then took a flitch of bacon off the wall, cut it into thick slices and covered Annie's body with fatty bacon so that it would burn away; yet this was never mentioned in the press. Most Worcestershire country folk know that fatty bacon has unusual properties, burning slowly and disappearing completely. In 1984 an elderly lady, Mrs Wall, was interviewed, who once lived in the rebuilt cottage. She said:

> The man who had lived in it before, he set fire to it. Well, he wanted to burn his wife. She was burned to death, you see, in the cottage. A flitch of bacon fell on her. He got it off the wall. My father, he was at Ombersley as a police sergeant, and he was ordered to keep the gaol open for him. My father searched with five constables and they found him smoking on the side of the road.

Be that as it may, Samuel seemed to have vanished. His description was telegraphed to all police stations in the area, but he was not seen. The police thought he might have committed suicide. The body of a man was found about five miles away at Wychbold. Samuel's son was unable to give a positive

On the right, projecting into the road, is the Fox and Goose *where the licensee did a roaring trade after the murder.* (Courtesy Alan Foxall)

identification, but Thomas Drew and the landlord of the *Fox and Goose* went over to look at the body and said it was definitely not Samuel's. Norgrove pool was dragged early on Sunday morning; again, nothing was found. He was at liberty some nineteen hours after the fire was discovered.

It was on the Saturday when a telephonic message arrived at Redditch saying that Samuel had been arrested in Trench Lane, on the road between Himbleton and Crowle, sitting on the side of the road in a drunken stupor. The man admitted that he was Samuel Middleton but denied all knowledge of the murder. He was so drunk that the police left him to sober up overnight before they brought him to Redditch police station and charged him. At midday on Monday, Samuel was brought before the magistrate at Redditch Police Court and charged with 'wilfully, maliciously and feloniously killing his wife, Annie Middleton, at Foxlydiate, on the morning of 10 May' and also with arson.

Overnight, Foxlydiate became famous. People flocked to see the burned ruins from as far away as Worcester and Birmingham. On the Saturday thousands came on foot, by bicycle or by horse-drawn vehicles. Even more arrived on the Sunday. Three police constables were set to guard the ruins. The landlord of the *Fox and Goose* made a small fortune.

Laid to Rest – a Saint and a Villain

Annie's funeral took place on Wednesday 12 May. She was to be buried on the western side of nearby Tardebigge churchyard. The route was lined with onlookers standing in respectful silence. At the church gates, the cortège was met by Canon Dickens; the vicar conducted the service but the canon performed the burial service.

The inquest was opened at the *Fox and Goose* on the Monday, but adjourned until the Thursday week, partly to allow time for the collection of evidence and partly because of the bank holiday. Laura Drew was the only witness. Samuel was remanded to Worcester until 21 May. There he was convicted and condemned.

During his imprisonment, he had only three visits. The first was a brief visit from his son. Then Samuel asked if he could see Mrs Drew, which surprised everyone as she had testified against him. Samuel told her that he was quite resigned to his fate. Mrs Drew asked him if he was guilty, to which he replied 'After you left, we went upstairs to bed. My wife continued nagging at me, and I got up and went downstairs with the intention of leaving the house, but she clung to me and stopped me from going, and I killed her. I hit her on the head with a poker.' His last visit was from his brother, Eli. The two brothers both had biblical names, Samuel and Eli.

Samuel was executed at Worcester on Tuesday, 15 July. Selected personnel were allowed to watch the execution, including the press, who reported that large doors were thrown open to reveal a place resembling a coach-house. A rope and noose hung from the beam over the drop, and the spot where Samuel was to stand was marked in chalk. At one minute to eight, Samuel appeared with a warder on each side and behind him a small procession, the governor of the gaol, the chaplain, the prison surgeon and a few others. Samuel was very pale as he approached the scaffold and he looked straight ahead without saying a word. His hands were already tied behind his back. The executioner strapped his legs together, put a cap over

Worcester prison, known as 'the Castle'. (Courtesy Family History Centre, Worcester)

his face and placed the noose round his neck. Shouting 'Stand back' to the onlookers, the executioner pulled the lever. Down went Samuel, with a dull thud. The chaplain recited a few words from the burial service, and, as the prisoner dropped, the prison bell began to toll.

CHAPTER 9

Murdered on Active Duty –
Wythall, Near Alvechurch

On the north-eastern tip of Redditch is the ancient village of Beoley. Centuries ago the villagers moved away, leaving only farmland with a few dwellings and the old church of St Leonard. The road northwards from Beoley crossroads still follows the line of the old Roman road, so narrow in places that cars need to pass singly. The steep banks are overgrown and the trees meet overhead. The lane is shaded in summer and is so dark at night that it is impossible to walk along it without a torch.

A shaft of sunlight illuminates the stone marking the place where PC Davies fell.

About half a mile east of Rowney Green the banks are steeper, and here, hidden in the undergrowth of the right-hand bank, is a memorial stone. It reads simply 'J.D. 1885'. This is the spot where a constable was murdered, probably the first policeman to be killed while on active duty.

Police Constable Davies

Police Constable James Davies of the Worcestershire Constabulary was a tall and powerful man, five feet ten inches tall and well built, as policemen were, back in 1885. Like his colleagues, he sported the regulation whiskers together with a light brown moustache. He was 34 years of age, married, with three young children and a heavily pregnant wife. In the force for five years, he had been transferred from Kidderminster, where he had a reputation for 'conscientious and unflinching discharge of his duty'. Later, his superiors were to describe him as 'a zealous and intelligent officer'.

Police constables were expected to serve nine hours out of every twenty-four, five hours of which were to be between the hours of 10 pm and 4 am. Davies therefore left his home in Beoley at ten o'clock on Friday, 27 February 1885. At one o'clock in the early morning he met the Wythall policeman at Portway, which was halfway between the two villages and about two miles north-east of Beoley. An hour later, they compared watches and separated. It was arranged that Davies should meet the Alvechurch constable at Rowney Green at four o'clock. Rowney Green was about a mile and a half north-west of Beoley. Davies had a two-and-a-half mile walk in front of him along a narrow country lane, crossing the Roman road near his destination.

POLICE-CONSTABLE DAVIES,

PC Davies. (Courtesy Alan Foxall)

Unfortunately, the Alvechurch constable was ill at home, and so Davies was not missed.

It was perhaps his 'conscientious and unflinching discharge of duty' that brought about his death, for, in the early hours in that dark lane, quite by accident, he came across a well-known poacher, Moses Shrimpton. A bright moon was shining that night and PC Davies evidently recognized him, then probably, in his usual conscientious and zealous manner asked to look inside his bag. Perhaps he tried to arrest him.

Moses Shrimpton

Moses Shrimpton was born in Long Crendon in Buckingham-shire in about 1820. He was five feet seven inches tall, well built and with a ruddy complexion. The Shrimpton family were needlemakers. They began to move from the workshops of Long Crendon to join the craftsmen of Redditch in about 1824. Their main business concern was Alfred Shrimpton & Sons, Britannia Works in William Street which made needles, fish hooks and fishing tackle, but they were a large family and other members were builders, publicans, coal merchants, drapers and grocers.

Moses Shrimpton. (Courtesy Alan Foxall)

It's puzzling how someone from such an affluent and well-established family can have such a long criminal record. Was he an alcoholic? Did he fall into bad company?

In about 1850, when Shrimpton was 30, he migrated to Redditch where he lodged with a 32-year-old widow, Mary Ann Mogg, and her 11-year-old son. Mary's previous husband had been a member of the Hemming family, another well-known and respected needle-making family. Ten years later they were man and wife with three children, Amelia, George and Thomas, aged 6, 4 and 1 respectively.

Shrimpton was described by various authorities as a fishing-tackle manufacturer, a needlemaker and a bricklayer, but his chosen profession was that of poacher, which landed him in prison for a few weeks nearly every year. When he was in his early forties his crimes became more serious. In 1862 he spent twenty-one days inside for assault. Three years later he was imprisoned for poaching and neglect of his family, three months on each charge. In 1868 he was sentenced to five years' penal servitude for maliciously inflicting grievous bodily harm on PC Haynes of Tardebigge. It is said that, had passers-by not intervened, PC Haynes would have died.

By 1885, Shrimpton was living in Birmingham with a certain Jane Moreton. They had been living at the *Star and Garter* in New Canal Street, a common beerhouse, but their drinking, shouting and quarrelling became a nuisance and they were asked to leave. About six weeks before the murder, the couple had moved to a run-down lodging house, number 9 Bartholomew Street. At their trial, the landlady claimed that they had told her they were man and wife. They occupied a garret at the top of the house and usually kept themselves to themselves. The couple spent most of the day in the garret, sending out for drink. As evening fell they emerged, wended their way to a public house and drank until they were turned out. They then returned to the attic, shouting and quarrelling until they fell asleep.

Shrimpton left the house in the evening once or twice a week, telling the landlady that he was off to work and that he would return between eight and nine the next morning. He always carried a bulky bag which he hid beneath his coat. He would come back in the morning, have a quick nap, then go out for an hour and a half and return the worse for wear. After these excursions the couple seemed to have plenty of money. His fellow-lodgers thought he must have a highly paid occupation as he only had to work at the most two nights a week and was able to spend money freely.

A Fight and a Murder
There is no doubt that there was a terrible fight in that dark lane in the early hours of the morning. Shrimpton was more

than 30 years older and three inches smaller than Davies, though he had one great advantage – an exceptionally sharp knife.

Late one evening sometime before the murder, Shrimpton had called in at the *Scale and Compass*, near Headless Cross, Redditch. A modern public house, *The Archers*, now stands on the site. The licensee happened to be the grandfather of the late Gilbert Hunt, who made cork fishing floats. Cork is very difficult to cut and so the family had acquired an expertise in producing sharp knives. The following was one of Gilbert's favourite stories:

> My granddad made knives for a hobby, all kinds of knives, kitchen knives, everything. One night, Moses Shrimpton called in for a drink. He had got one of those long leather cricket bags and he had been down at Rushy Bottom (along the Feckenham Road at Headless Cross) where he had pinched some fowl. He put his bag on the table. My grandad said, 'What have you got there, Mo?' and Moses said, 'Some fowl.' My granddad then sold Moses a knife.

The knife in question had a bone handle and two blades, one being about five or six inches long and having a sharp point.

The nearest farm was two fields away and some time between three-thirty and four o'clock on Saturday morning the farm's watchdog began barking furiously.

About half past eight that morning, John Twigg, a farmer from Rowney Green, was going to work when he came across the body of the policeman. The officer was lying obliquely across the road, his feet in the gutter at the foot of a high bank while his head was resting in the middle of the road, in a large pool of blood. There were terrible wounds to his face, neck and hands. On the right side of his face was a long cut from the chin to the ear, completely dividing the cheek and there was a stab wound through the right side of the neck which would have caused death, but not immediately. The throat had been carefully cut from left to right so deeply that the windpipe was exposed. He had obviously used his hands to

The dark and lonely lane where the murder took place.

ward off the knife, so that the first finger of the left hand was severed above the middle joint and hung by a piece of skin, and two fingers on the right hand were nearly cut off. The left thumb was also cut.

Farmer Twigg ran to the nearest farmhouse and raised the alarm. The Wythall policeman came over – perhaps on his bicycle – and arranged for the body to be taken to a local wheelwright's, who happened to have room in his shed. There the body remained until the inquest.

About 200 yards from the body in the direction of Beoley crossroads was a police whistle. Policemen were taught to put the whistle between their teeth so that they could leave both hands free to secure the prisoner or protect themselves. PC Davies could have therefore dropped the whistle accidentally when and if he spoke to Shrimpton.

That night, six fowl had been stolen from a nearby farm. Footprints went from the fowl-house across several fields to a gate halfway between the crossroads and the body. The footprints were those of nailed boots; the nails were later found to correspond to Shrimpton's boots. Near the body was a second set of footprints, said to be those of PC Davies.

The two men therefore seem to have met 200 yards from where Davies was murdered. Another strange fact is that Davies still had the handcuffs in his pocket. No one knows what happened between those 200 yards and the murder site, since Shrimpton protested his innocence to the end.

Around the body were signs of a vicious struggle. Nearby was an oak stick with blood and hairs sticking to it. Whether this was Shrimpton's staff or Davies's truncheon is not clear. The grass on the bank had been flattened by the shape of a figure and spattered with blood. It appeared that Davies had reeled back from the stab wound to his neck on to the bank. His attacker had then kneeled over him and, as he lay dying, carefully slit his throat.

The right hand was clenched, and on prizing it open, they saw that it contained a quantity of his own whiskers. He must have put his hand up to his face at the first cut. Near the body were several fowl's feathers. Davies's watch was missing.

Arrested by Telegraph
Superintendent Jeffry, of the Bromsgrove Division, rushed to the scene as soon as he heard the news. When he was told that some fowl had been stolen nearby, he immediately suspected Shrimpton, who had stolen fowl from the farm on a previous occasion.

The police of that time used a telegraph system whereby messages could be transmitted either by a series of taps in Morse code, or by a machine that perforated dots on to a strip of paper at the receiving end. The paper was then fed into a machine and, as each group of dots referred to a letter, the message could be read. In this way, information could be relayed from one station to another in a matter of minutes. Jeffry immediately telegraphed all the police divisions in the neighbourhood. It so happened that Superintendent Tyler at Kings Heath had a photograph of Shrimpton, and, knowing that the suspect lived somewhere in Birmingham, he took the photograph to Detective Inspector Stroud in Moor Street in the centre of Birmingham. The rural areas around Birmingham had been plagued with an epidemic of fowl-stealing that coincided with the periods when Shrimpton was released from gaol, so Detective Inspector Stroud had been keeping an eye on him for some time.

Shrimpton and Jane Moreton woke up in the morning to find two burly policemen standing over them, Inspector Stroud and Superintendent Tyler. Stroud caught hold of Moses as he went to get out of bed and snapped the handcuffs on him. Jane was told to get dressed, and each garment was carefully searched before she put it on. In the pocket of her skirt was a large pocket knife. The two blades had been washed but at the joint were traces of blood. The sleeve of Shrimpton's overcoat had been washed but it had not been possible to remove all the blood that covered his right arm from the wrist to the elbow. His hat, a low-crowned felt hat, had also been washed. The front of his knitted woollen shirt was splashed with blood and his boots had been carefully cleaned and greased.

Shrimpton himself looked as if he had been in a fight. To the left of his forehead was a cut about one and a half inches long, and there was a smaller cut to the left and to his ear. These could have been made with a police truncheon. Asked how he had received his wounds, he replied, 'I got them about a week ago by falling down in Ludgate Hill, drunk.' Sticking plaster had been put over the wounds and blood was still seeping out from the largest cut.

Back in Beoley, hundreds flocked to the dark lane where PC Davies had met his death. Throughout Sunday the road was blocked for half a mile, although there was nothing to see except a patch of bloodstained sand.

The funeral of PC Davies took place in St Leonard's Church at Beoley. Representatives of the police force came from across the whole country and as far away as Scotland and Wales. Horse-drawn vehicles stretched for half a mile along the road by the *Village Inn*.

The inquest was held at the *Coach and Horses*, Weatheroak Hill, and the inquiry was held at the *Red Lion Hotel*, Alvechurch. Sales of the *Redditch Indicator* soared. The journalists' fortunes were further enhanced later by the sale of photographs of Davies's gravestone at one shilling each.

Jane Moreton and the Watch

Jane was about 40 years of age, and although the wife of a Redditch bricklayer, she had been living with Shrimpton for some years.

After moving to Birmingham, she became friendly with the wife of a brewer, Mrs Facer, and helped her with some housework. It will be remembered that PC Davies's watch was missing. On the Saturday, Jane went to see Mrs Facer, produced an old-fashioned German silver watch and offered to sell it to her for two shillings. Mrs Facer offered her one shilling, which Jane accepted. Later in the day, Mrs Facer offered the watch to a young man for five shillings. The young man did not want it himself, but said he would try to sell it for her. He took it to a public house at the corner of Lawley Street and Great Brook Street and passed it round. As no one wanted the watch he returned it to Mrs Facer.

One of the young men in the public house read a description of the stolen watch in the newspaper, noticed the similarity and notified the police. Mrs Facer said that she no longer had the watch and described it quite differently, but, after questioning, she broke down. She confessed that she had given the watch to her husband to dispose of, as she suspected that it had been stolen. The police raced to Mr Facer's place of employment, the malthouse in Heneage Street, but it was too late: the watch had been thrown into the furnace. The fire was allowed to die out and the ashes were raked, but there was no sign of the watch. Mr Facer was arrested and brought before the borough justices at the Public Office, charged with being an accessory after the fact.

Shrimpton and his lover were arrested and charged by Superintendent Tyler. Shrimpton stated, 'I know nothing at all about it. I can prove where I was on Friday night. It is no use saying anything here. I will say what I have got to say in another place' (meaning the Assizes). Jane looked very nervous and said, 'God in heaven knows, I know nothing at all about it.' Shrimpton was put in the cells adjoining the police court and Jane was taken to Balsall Heath Police Station.

They were both tried by Baron Huddlestone at Worcester Assizes on 6 May. Shrimpton looked grey and gaunt in the dock. He had lost weight and the ruddy cheeks were now pale. He looked like a harmless little old man. When pronouncing the death sentence, the judge added,

> It is said that you are an old man. At all events you are not so old as many in this Court. You may have time to make amends to the Almighty Being whom you have offended and I beg of you to use carefully the time which is left to you in this world.

As for Jane, the judge pointed out that, under the laws of the day, if she had been married to Shrimpton she could not have been charged, so that the jury would be justified in returning a verdict of not guilty. And so she was set free.

Apart from the prison chaplain, Shrimpton had no visitors. He asked to see his son and son-in-law, who came together and stayed for half an hour. When he saw them he began to weep, but soon regained his composure.

Justice is Done

Shrimpton had been allowed nineteen days 'to make amends to the Almighty Being' and was hung on 25 May 1885. The day of the execution was grey and wet. Shrimpton was allowed to dress himself in his own clothes, instead of the prison garb.

The County Gaol had been built in Salt Lane in 1813 in the style of a medieval castle; accordingly, the name of the road had been changed to Castle Street. Until Shrimpton arrived, temporary scaffolds were erected, but it was then decided to build a permanent scaffold with a brick-lined pit about nine feet deep. Over the pit was a trapdoor and at the side of the pit was a lever that had to be swung across to open the trap. Hanging needed precise calculations on the drop so that the victim would be killed without the head being torn off. His executioner was a well-known professional, James Berry. He arrived by train on the Saturday, wearing a smart suit, looking more like a business executive. Shrimpton was his twenty-sixth execution and he had used the same rope for twenty of the hangings. At eight o'clock Berry fastened Shrimpton's wrists together in front of him. The condemned man walked the fifty yards to the gallows in a

James Berry, the executioner.

procession. First came the chaplain in his surplice, reading the words of the burial service, then came Shrimpton with the executioner at his side. In the procession were the under-sheriff for the county, the prison governor, medical officer and chief warder, two acting principal warders and representatives of the magistracy and the Press. When the gallows were reached, the chaplain paused in his reading and Shrimpton took up his position above the drop. The executioner strapped his feet together, put a white bag over his face and adjusted the rope. As the chaplain intoned, 'In the midst of life we are in death', the lever was drawn and Shrimpton dropped into the pit.

The executioner had calculated a drop of nine feet from Shrimpton's weight of ten stone, but he had failed to allow for the thinner skin of an older man. As if in divine retribution for the slitting of Davies's neck, the flesh on Shrimpton's throat had been torn open from ear to ear so that the windpipe was exposed.

Outside the prison a crowd of about 2,000 had collected. As soon as the execution was completed, a black flag was flown over the entrance and the bell of the prison chapel tolled. The executioner left the prison on foot to get to Worcester station, accompanied by a large mob.

A fund was established for the widow of PC Davies and his children, and the donations were generous. Even today, flowers are left by several people on the constable's grave on each anniversary of his death.

CHAPTER 10

The Lovers' Pact – Redditch and Northfield

This is a murder unlike any other. It came about not through rage or jealousy or hate, but through passionate love. In 1941, the Merry family were living at 205 Hewell Road, Redditch. There were five young children, the eldest 14 and the youngest just 1 year old. Their father, Harold, was 40 years of age, a fair-haired man of average height.

Their neighbour, Maurice Clarke, knew the family well:

The Harold Merry that I knew, when a boy living in Lodge Road in the years before the war, was a quiet, likeable, family-man. At that time he worked for the old SWS Electricity Company in Smallwood Street, Redditch. The house in which his family lived was a peculiar place, built originally as the office of a local building company, Millwards, whose workshops were in the next street. It had no garden and the Merry family lived in what had once been the upstairs office.

Occasionally, his children came to play in our garden, which was only three doors away; I especially remember their oldest daughter, Margaret, who was about my age. She died tragically of diphtheria in the mid-1930s. Not long afterwards, the family moved down to the Batchley Estate to begin what they hoped would be a new life.

Sadly, this was not to be of lasting happiness; with the coming of the war in September 1939 a train of events was set in motion which would lead ultimately to almost unbearable misery for the family, and for Harold the gallows.

Lodge Road. Harold Merry lived here in a first-floor apartment for many years.

In July 1941, Harold Merry was transferred to more important war work and became a sheet metal inspector at the Aero Works based in the Austin Motor Company at Longbridge. He soon became involved with 27-year-old Joyce Dixon, who had been working at the factory for three years as a shorthand typist. She was very efficient and earning £3 a

Harold Merry was living here in Hewell Road when he made the suicide pact.

week, which was a good wage – many men in 1941 were only earning £4 a week. She lived with her mother, a widow, at 8 Rowans Way, Northfield. Joyce had had a nervous breakdown as a result of overwork and was a resident in a Rubery mental institution from July 1931 to February 1932. She returned to the mental home from December 1935 to January 1937. She was then discharged and said to be completely cured.

Harold began taking her to the pictures and after only six weeks they realized that they were both very much in love. Harold had neglected to tell Joyce that he was married with five children, but she was informed of this fact in September by Harold's foreman.

Harold visited Joyce's home seven times and was introduced to her mother. Neither Joyce nor Harold mentioned that he was a married man. In the strict sexual code of the 1940s, going out with a married man was a cardinal sin.

In September 1941 Joyce wrote a passionate love letter to Harold, which was opened by his wife. As a result he was locked out of the house and went to live with his sister, Lily Price, at 44 Mount Pleasant, Redditch. He seems to have had a very accommodating wife, as once a week he went home to have a bath and change his underclothes. His sister was not at all happy about the relationship with Joyce and told him that he was to end it before Christmas.

In mid-March 1942 Harold went to see Joyce's mother and asked if she had any objections to their getting engaged as they 'understood each other'. Again, he failed to mention that he was already married. He said that he was going to London on business and staying at the home of the parents of his niece's boyfriend. He asked permission to take Joyce with him in order to choose an engagement ring. The mother's reply was that they were old enough to know right from wrong and although he was nearly old enough to be her daughter's father, she had no objection if he could make her happy. The night before he went to London Harold slept at his wife's house. He told her, too, that he was off to London on business with his boss.

There was, of course, no business trip and no niece's boyfriends' parents. The couple stayed in a hotel in Bloomsbury

Street as Mr and Mrs Merry. While they were enjoying illicit bliss in London, Harold's supervisor called to see Joyce's mother and informed her that Harold was married; and so when they returned home on Friday, 27 March, Mrs Dixon confronted the couple with the fact that she now knew the truth. Harold denied being married but said he had had to tell his employers at Austin's that he had a wife, otherwise they would not have given him a job. Mrs Dixon said at the trial that the explanation 'didn't wash' with her. She told Joyce to work overtime on the Saturday and Sunday to keep her occupied but, of course, Harold objected to the idea. Harold was out of favour with his sister because he had told her he would be back earlier, so he slept downstairs in his long-suffering wife's house.

The couple met on the Saturday morning, when Joyce was very upset about her mother's attitude. That night, Harold stayed in his wife's house again.

The Suicide Pact

On Sunday, 29 March, Joyce left her home at 3.45 pm telling her mother she was going to meet Harold. She said that he owed her some money and she was hoping to get it back.

The following is an account of the events based on Harold's statement at the trial. In his original statement at the inquest he did not make quite so many attempts to persuade Joyce to return home.

They went to Quinton Park, where Joyce tearfully complained that her mother kept asking her questions about what had occurred in London. She said she thought her mother was losing her love for her and she could not carry on much longer telling her mother lies. Harold said that her mother would forgive her, but Joyce replied, 'You don't know, you don't understand.' Joyce said, 'We cannot get married, but if we could die together it would help.' According to his own account, Harold said, 'No, we don't want to do that, there are thousands who have done wrong as we have, let's have some chocolate and an orange' – these were left over from their London trip. Harold suggested that they composed a suicide letter. He brought out his pocket notebook and wrote:

Joyce and I have been living as man and wife at 36 Bloomsbury Street, London, hoping that I should be able to get a divorce. We have been trying to keep it away from Joyce's mother, Mrs Dixon, but Joyce's foreman went and told Mrs Dixon I was married. So we find it impossible to carry on much longer. So we are going to die together because we are terribly in love with each other. We were going to London to live after the holidays, and find some work, but since Joyce's foreman told Mrs Dixon it has upset our plans. Joyce herself knows I was married. I told her myself, also Mr Taylor, my foreman, told her last September and for God's sake forgive her. She is so happy now. She knows we are going to die together. So goodbye all.

He read it out to Joyce who, said Harold, agreed with it and signed it, despite there being no mention of Harold needing forgiveness. Harold remarked, 'I suppose when we get home we will have changed our minds,' to which Joyce replied, 'Yes, I suppose we will.'

They reached Hawkesley Crescent near her home at about nine o'clock. Fifteen minutes later, after a passionate embrace, he wished her goodnight. He had gone about twenty yards when Joyce called him back and said, 'I am not going home.' He said, 'Let me come home with you and explain everything to your mother.' She said she could not allow him to do that. They decided to go across the fields and die together, but they had not decided how they were going to die. He again pleaded with the girl to go home.

They reached a stile where they had never been before, where Joyce said, 'Come on, let's die together.' Again he pleaded with her to go home. She did not agree, so he pulled a necktie out of his case and put it round her neck. He always carried a spare necktie so that he could change it in the evening. Two or three seconds later she asked him to pull it tight. Harold said, 'I was hoping she would come to her senses and go home, but she helped me to pull it tight and it broke in my hands.' He continued:

I had decided that I was going to die with her. The girl was standing with her back to the stile and as the tie broke she slid to the ground. I bent down to pick her up and she said, 'Listen, I can hear voices, let's go into the other field, it's more private.' As there was a gap at the bottom of the stile I dragged her through into the other field. She was conscious and said, 'I love you, I love you.' When she said that my nerves gave way and I bent down to pick her up. I did not intend to kill myself after that.

I said to her, 'Joyce, let's go home to your mother.' She said, 'No, you don't understand.' I told her that I was going to fetch her mother myself. I tried to get her on her feet but she would not let me, although she was able to get up. I left her and went over to the stile, hoping that she would follow as she had done previously, and I could take her home. I stood by the hedge to see if anyone was about because Joyce had heard a voice. I stood there from ten to fifteen minutes and then I went back to where I had left her. She had disappeared. About two yards from the bank of the pool I saw something, and I ran and shouted, 'Come out of the pool.' I went into the pool and picked her up. She gave no sign of life and I realized she was dead. Then I pulled my tie out of my collar, put it round my neck and pulled it. I was standing in the pool. As I pulled the tie it broke and I went dazed. I fell face downwards in the pool and when I came to, I said, 'Joyce, where are you?' I stayed in the water some time and then I went to the bank to have a cigarette. After I had smoked it I went into the water again to do myself in. I let myself go face downwards into the water. Then a picture came into my mind of my children and a voice said, 'Don't do it.' I tried to drag the girl out but by her weight I realized she was dead. I came out of the pool between 4.50 and 5 am, I asked a passing postman the time.

He then went to his wife's house.

At seven-thirty early the next morning, Joyce's brother, Victor Dixon, received a telephone call from his mother saying that Joyce had gone for a walk on Sunday afternoon and had not returned. Victor rang the factory and discovered that neither Harold nor Joyce had turned up for work.

Harold Confesses

He went to Harold's house in Hewell Road. Mrs Merry opened the door and shouted upstairs to Harold that he was wanted. A bumping noise came from the front bedroom, Mr Dixon ran upstairs and found Harold standing by the washstand with some electric switch cord tied round his neck several times. Dixon unwound the cord and asked Harold where his sister was. Harold said, 'I will take you to her.' Dixon then said, 'You have murdered her.' Harold replied, 'That's right, she's in the brook in the field at the back of the house.' Dixon drove Harold to Redditch Police Station and told the inspector that Harold had murdered his sister. PC Albert Morris was in the police station when Harold was brought in. Harold was white-faced and dithering from the cold. The constable was amazed to hear Harold's story as he had known him for twenty years and he had been a respectable, law-abiding citizen. He wondered if he was having a mental breakdown, but noted that he seemed to be quite rational.

Harold was cautioned. He said, 'All I can say is that I am guilty.' The bottom of his jacket was wet and he had green 'seeds' (probably duck weed) adhering to it and the shoulders were damp. One of his fingers was bleeding and there was a red mark round his neck. Harold explained that when he heard Dixon talking to his wife he had tried to hang himself in his bedroom.

When he was searched, three letters from Joyce were found containing such statements as 'I love you so terribly' and 'I love you with all my heart' and 'Oh I do love you my sweet'. The suicide pact was found in a notebook in the inside breast pocket of his jacket. The cover was slightly damp but many pages were quite dry. Harold told the constables, 'That is the letter I wrote, you will see that we have both signed it … At the end we agreed to end our lives together but the water was not deep enough for me. I know that she is dead. She was in the water all night.' He said that he had parted from his wife (not mentioning that he had just come from her house) and added, 'We were happy until I met Miss Dixon.' A wedding ring was found later.

He stated that he had offered to kill Joyce first, saying to her, 'I promise faithfully I will die with you', adding, 'faithfully I did not keep'. He omitted to say this at the trial; instead, he told the court that he had pleaded with the girl to go home. His original version of the killing was, 'After strangling the girl I pulled my necktie tight and fell in the water dazed. I shouted, "Joyce, where are you?". I got up and made another attempt to kill myself. I stayed in the water till about 4.30 am.' This differs slightly from his statement at the trial, and as for the water not being deep enough, it is possible to drown in three inches of water. Only the bottom of his jacket had duckweed on it and his upper half was merely damp. If he had put his face in the water it was a very quick dip. Perhaps the officers did not believe his story because they then went to Harold's home to find his muddy trousers and other clothes.

Today the police would have been on the scene of the crime within twenty minutes. This was 1942, and Superintendent Richardson and Inspector George Brown from the Birmingham police force did not reach the site until 2.45 pm. Harold took them to a pond at Turves Green Farm, Northfield, where they found Joyce's body floating face downwards. The body was fully clothed except for the hat and shoes.

Three days later Harold stated, 'I have thought it over, and I want to say I am not guilty now.'

He appeared at Birmingham police court on Thursday, 9 April 1942 and was accused, charged and remanded until 23 April. The inquest was adjourned until 29 July but on 17 July he came before Birmingham Assizes.

Professor James Webster, Director of the West Midlands Forensic Laboratory had been in charge of the post-mortem. A brilliant pathologist, he had reconstructed the remains of 'Bella' found in the wych-elm at Hagley. He mentioned that Joyce was not pregnant and stated that death was asphyxia from drowning, but she had been brought very near to death by strangling before the immersion. She was unconscious when she entered the water. Cross-examined by Harold's counsel, Mr J F Bourke, Dr Webster said it was not beyond possibility that Miss Dixon was conscious when she was first immersed in the water, but it was not beyond theoretical possibility to fly to the moon, although he doubted its practicability. His opinion, from indications, was that she was

Thomas Pierrepoint, the hangman.

unconscious and he had never had any doubts on this point. That silenced Mr Bourke.

The judge, Mr Justice Croome-Johnson, made several rather improper remarks. He snapped at Harold, 'Don't smile about it, this is a serious matter', and to the prosecution he remarked, 'Haven't you asked enough questions?'

Mr Bourke said that there were three possible verdicts, wilful murder, attempted murder and not guilty. There was no doubt that Harold was a bad, immoral man; but for him the young woman would be alive today. At this, Harold began to weep for the first time during the trial. Mr Bourke asked the jury to return a verdict of attempted murder. Instead, the verdict was returned as wilful murder. Harold stood calm and unemotional when this was announced, but there were hysterical outbursts from the well of the court and the public gallery. He was to be hanged at Birmingham on 10 September 1942.

There was a tremendous public outcry. Maurice Clarke, their neighbour, remembers it well:

Following the verdict of wilful murder there came, in Redditch, a fierce public reaction to what seemed to be a totally unjust decision. Most people were concerned about the effects upon Harold's long-suffering wife and her children. Efforts were made to save Harold for the sake of the family. Others felt it wrong to charge him with killing his lover in what seemed to be a suicide pact.

A petition of 2,000 signatures seeking a reprieve was forwarded to the Home Secretary but rejected.

These tragic events took place more than sixty years ago, and I sincerely hope that Harold's family have long since found peace of mind in coming to terms with a fate in which they were the innocent victims, and which the people of Redditch have all but forgotten.

Harold was drawn into the system of judicial killing which would lead to his coming, in the last moments of his life, face to face with his executioner, Thomas Pierrepoint, in the grim execution chamber of Winson Green prison, Birmingham.

The instrument of Harold's nemesis, Thomas Pierrepoint, was one of a family of hangmen, who retired as chief executioner in 1946 having hanged 294 prisoners in his time. His brother, Henry, lost his position as chief executioner in 1910 after he arrived drunk at Chelmsford prison to hang a condemned man there.

Henry's son, Albert, the most prolific hangman in the family, followed his Uncle Tom's dictum, 'If you can't do it without whisky, don't do it at all.' He successfully combined his job as a publican with that of a hangman, and soberly hung more than 400 convicted murderers.

Like the trial judges who generally enjoyed a good lunch after condemning their quota of unfortunates to be hanged, Albert looked forward to a good cigar.

Poor Harold had joined the ranks of the innumerable men who have come to an unfortunate end because of their passion for a woman. They litter the pages of our history books, for example, Samson and Delilah, Henry VIII and Anne Boleyn, Edward VIII and Wallis Simpson. In our own times eminent politicians frequently fall from grace because of an illicit relationship. No one explains the circumstances better than Robert Graves (1895–1985) in his poem 'Symptoms of Love':

Love is a universal migraine
A bright stain on the vision
Blotting out reason.

CHAPTER 11

Friends and Enemies – Evesham

By a strange geological quirk, the River Avon makes a large loop in the south-east corner of Worcestershire. It is in this loop that the little town of Evesham has developed, with the river on its eastern, southern and western sides. It was also here that a swineherd saw such an astonishing vision that he reported it to Bishop Egwin of Worcester, who decided to found a monastery there. This is now only a small ruin, but the bell tower is still standing and the beautiful old Almonry once belonging to the monastery has been turned into a museum and tourist information centre.

Simon de Montfort camped here with his army in 1265, thinking that he could not be attacked with a river on three sides. Instead, he found he was trapped. His army was routed and he was killed, his body hacked to pieces; his remains are buried in Evesham's Abbey Park, beneath a small memorial.

Evesham had a history of kicking against authority in religious matters. In the 1530s a bitter struggle arose between Henry VIII and the kindly old abbot, who, despite the strong possibility of losing his head, steadfastly refused to surrender his monastery. The king acquired the monastery in 1537 by trickery.

In 1410, more than a century before the monastery was dissolved, Evesham provided a religious martyr, unique in that he was not a priest or a bishop, merely an ordinary working-class tailor. In those days Roman Catholics believed that, when the bread and wine were given at the sacrament, the bread and wine actually changed into the flesh and blood of Christ. Iohn Badby of Evesham said that the bread was merely holy bread, and was not transformed. He was dragged before the Bishop of Worcester who handed him over to the Archbishop of Canterbury and the Bishop of London. They passed him to the secular authorities, who condemned him to be burned to death at Smithfield in London. A huge bonfire was built. Badby was taken there, put inside an empty barrel and placed on the bonfire. The bonfire was lit, and Badby cried out for mercy. Watching this procedure was the Prince of Wales. He ordered the barrel to be removed and promised Badby a yearly allowance from the royal treasury if he would recant. Badby refused, was put back on the pyre and was burned to death.

What culture persuaded him to stand against the bishops and sacrifice his life in such a way? No doubt he was remembered in Evesham through succeeding generations, inspiring others to make sacrifices in the cause of their beliefs.

The next hundred years were particularly difficult times. The nation saw the reign of Bloody Mary, an ardent Roman Catholic, then that of Elizabeth I, who promoted the Anglican Church. The following years saw Charles I beheaded and the terrible first Civil War of 1642–6. The great Puritan, Oliver Cromwell, as leader of the country, was fairly tolerant towards new sects – but not so the local authorities. In 1642 a Grand Jury declared they would defend the Protestant religion against 'Popish recusants (Roman Catholics), Anabaptists and all other separatists'. This included the Quakers.

Properly, the Quakers should be called 'Friends' but earned their nickname because of the way that they shook with emotion when speaking. The movement began in the middle of the 1600s, when some felt that the ruling Protestants had lost the true spirit of Christianity. The founder is generally said to be George Fox (1624–91), a Leicestershire man, son of a weaver. In 1648 he began to preach in public and by 1658 communities were established throughout England.

George Fox, said to be the founder of the Quaker movement.

Quakers at Evesham
No one knows when the Friends were first established at Evesham, but by 1655, a century after Henry VIII had snatched the monastery, they were meeting just across the river in Bengeworth at

the house of Thomas Cartwright. Like Badby, they were the ordinary men of the town, traders and labourers. A curious fact is that although Quakers are firm pacificists and refuse to take part in 'bloody principles and practices', Cartwright and another four founder members of the group had all fought in the parliamentary army during the Civil War. Perhaps the terrible experiences of war had converted them to pacifism.

Their mentor and inspiration was the evangelist Humphrey Smith, from Little Cowarn in Herefordshire. He, too, had fought in the parliamentary army and afterwards became a popular public preacher. He travelled round England, drawing great crowds. He had gone through much suffering for his cause, he had been imprisoned, scourged, stripped naked and flogged before a crowd and nearly died in a filthy prison in Winchester. In 1655 he came to the town and held meetings 'in private'.

There were other sects (such as the Anabaptists) and denominations (such as the Roman Catholics) meeting in Evesham, but none were persecuted in the same way as the Friends. To some extent, it was their own fault. Other separatists

The old Bridge Street in Evesham; the western end touches Bengeworth.

held their meetings secretly; not so the Quakers. They advertised their services and sometimes even held them in the open air, where everyone could see and join in. One male Quaker ran naked through the streets to illustrate an obscure theological point. Another Quaker declared she could raise the dead, and so a group of Friends went to Claines churchyard, just outside Worcester, and a corpse was dug up for her. She stood over it, praying and urging, but nothing happened.

The Friends believe that every person holds a direct line to God, and that vicars, rectors and priests are unnecessary. This did not please the local vicar, the Reverend Hopkins, who was minister of All Saints' from 1642 to 1662. In 1655 Hopkins held forth during a service, ranting and raving about the Friends and whipping up anti-Friend hysteria. His entire congregation – numbering several hundred – marched to Bengeworth where the Quakers were holding a service. The situation was nasty. The crowd stood outside the house for several hours, shouting insults and throwing mud at the windows. The Quakers remained quiet and calm and eventually the crowd dispersed.

That same evening constables arrived and arrested the two leaders, Humphrey Smith and Thomas Cartwright, and took them off to the local Justice. The two men were released but told to report back the next morning. That night, the authorities sat plotting to find some law under which they could imprison the Friends. Then they remembered that the Quakers will never swear an oath; so the authorities decided to ask them to swear the oath of abjuration supporting the government. The Friends refused to swear and the authorities were able to act.

Smith and Cartwright were taken to the gaoler's house. The following evening the JPs and the constables arrived and asked the gaoler why he hadn't beaten the prisoners with his staff. A crowd gathered outside, shouting for the Friends. Humphrey began to preach to them out of a window, but in the crowd was a JP called Robert Martin, who began to whoop. The crowd took up this gesture and began throwing dirt and stones. The window was broken and Martin pulled Humphrey out of the window. The lives of the two men were saved by a magistrate and former mayor, Captain Pitway, who, on seeing 'the rage of the people' declared, 'The prisoners shall not go forth this night. If thou has anything to do with them, thou mayst do it in the morning'. Pitway later joined the Society of Friends.

Humphrey Smith was sent to the dungeon, a filthy, dark, close hole. He afterwards wrote a description of it. It was not twelve feet square and there was one hole four inches wide through which to take in food and straw. There were no toilet facilities. Prisoners were forced to burn a candle every day as it was so dark and because of the smell of the dung and urine.

The following Sunday, 28 August, a meeting was arranged with Friends, JPs and Officers. Friends who came to attend the meeting were put in the stocks. On 9 September, Smith was hauled away to the dungeon again. Robert Martin JP told the warders to knock anyone who was standing round the entrance to the dungeon into the dungeon hole and throw dirt on them. He set eight men with weapons to make sure no one approached the hole, four on each side.

In the 1600s, books were rare and of great value. All the books belonging to the Quakers, sixty copies, were taken and burned in the market place.

Fifty inhabitants signed a paper complaining about the treatment of the Friends, intending it to be sent to Oliver Cromwell, but Humphrey Smith, on his release, angered the authorities by printing and circulating it. As the pamphlet was said to be libellous the Friends were sent for trial in Evesham before Robert Atkyns, son of the Baron of the Exchequer. They could have stated their case and perhaps won friends in high places, but instead, they annoyed the judge by refusing to take their hats off, to demonstrate that they did not believe in a superior authority. Smith was fined £5, the others £3 and the lesser followers £2. The printers of the pamphlet were fined £4. Captain Pitway, who had saved their lives a few days previously, was also brought before the court. He was fined £20, an enormous sum, and stripped of his office. The sheriff took away goods from several friends and confiscated a larger amount than the warrant allowed. This reached the ears of Oliver Cromwell, who ordered that their goods be restored.

In the October, a new mayor was elected, Edmund Young. He was determined to stamp out the Quakers. He marched into a Quaker meeting with his officers and said it was an unlawful assembly, since more than eight were present. He and his men pulled, pushed and kicked the Quakers. Smith and two others were thrown into the dungeon, while one woman and six men were put in the stocks. The other men were imprisoned at four separate places across Evesham. Some were kept at the gaoler's house, who charged them an extortionate rate for lodging and food. Eight refused to pay, so they went to the main gaol, above the dungeon. Several joined the three men in the dungeon.

None of the prisoners were allowed candles, even those in the dungeon. After several days and nights the mayor sent a slice of bread and a small glass of beer to each prisoner, saying it was a prisoner's ration; but they refused the offering. A hole led from the dungeon up into the street, and people could not bear to go near it because of the smell of excrement from below. The mayor made a trapdoor into the dungeon and took away bedding and bedclothes that had been sent in. A Friend

The old stocks are carefully preserved in front of the Almonry.

brought straw but the mayor would not allow the door to be opened. Another Friend asked if he could remove the dung, and was put in the stocks just for asking. One man kept in the dungeon was so ill that he was turned out into the night. Some of the prisoners lay for several days 'like men asleep'. The three ringleaders were kept in the dungeon for fourteen weeks.

A couple of travellers heard about the plight of the Friends and went to see the gaoler to ask him about their condition. The gaoler invited them to visit the prisoners, then locked the door and refused to let them out until they had paid him a substantial fee. Another Friend, who just happened to be visiting Evesham, was put in the stocks on a freezing cold night, then forced out of the town. He boldly returned, and asked the mayor what offence he had committed. The mayor put him in the stocks again.

A Friend in London, Mary Clark, heard about the treatment of her colleagues and travelled to Evesham to expostulate with the mayor. Before she had finished her tirade, he pushed her out of his shop and put her in the stocks for three hours on a busy market day.

The tribulations of the Evesham Friends came to the ears of George Fox, thought to be the founder of the movement, and one dark night he slipped quietly into Evesham. The next morning, he visited the prisoners to give them some encouragement. Unfortunately, as he was leaving the town, he was recognized by a magistrate who raised the alarm, but Fox jumped on his horse and managed to get away.

Persecuted to Death

On 17 November, two women Friends named Margaret Newby and Elizabeth Courten (or Quorte) came to Evesham and held a meeting in Pitway's house. After the meeting, they visited the prisoners. As they were returning, the mayor seized them and put them in the stocks. They were placed in the room over the dungeon in stocks made for hands and feet, and the holes for the hands were too small. The mayor visited them to make sure that they were really uncomfortable. They were in the stocks for fifteen hours, then the mayor sent them out of the town on a freezing night. Margaret Newby died soon afterwards.

The present frontage to the Friends' meeting house.

When the prisoners returned home they were ruined men. They suffered from poor health for the rest of their lives. They had lost their jobs and no one dared employ them. The trades of those who were self-employed had died out because of their long absence.

The persecution of the Friends continued for thirty years. On 13 December 1662 Major Wild came to Evesham and ordered the Friends to appear before him. They were told to appear at Worcester the next day, and all did so except Richard Walker, a poor sick man, over 60 years old. Soldiers drove him on foot before their horses and when he could go no further, they dragged him along by force. The major even trampled on him with his horse and threatened to shoot him. At length they set him on horseback and brought him to Worcester gaol. Walker

Friends' meeting house, with a pathway leading to the older, rear section.

died soon after his committal. He was a man of meek, innocent and Christian spirit, inoffensive in life and conversation, and generally regarded with affection by those that knew him.

There is a sequel to this story. In 2001 sales staff working in Priceless Shoes in the centre of Evesham reported that there had been strange incidents in the shop. Stock was put away each night but in the morning, when they opened up the shop, shoes and boxes were scattered about. The fire alarm went off in the early hours of each morning. A ladder was moved from one side of the shop to the other when the shop was closed over the Christmas period. The manager's mobile phone was dialled from the shop after the staff had all gone home.

To see if they could throw any light on the matter, the staff of Priceless Shoes went down the road to see the historians at the tourist information centre, based in the old Almonry, to find the history of the building. Below the shop was a cellar, and research by the historians revealed that below that cellar was another room – the old dungeon, where the Friends had suffered three and a half centuries earlier.

CHAPTER 12

The Brothers Grim – Wood Norton, Near Evesham

This chapter tells the story of two brothers who were hung on the same day for the same murder which, perhaps, neither of them committed.

The year was 1889. At that time, there was only a small middle class, and a great divide existed between those who were wealthy and those who were poor. A working man, especially those at the lower end of the social scale, such as farm labourers, earned a miserable wage that barely covered rent and food; there was nothing left for extras such as clothes and bedding. The wealthy, by contrast, led very comfortable lives.

Among the super rich of Evesham was the duc d'Orléans, claimant to the throne of France. In 1857 the fourth son of the exiled Louis-Philippe, the last king of France, had arrived in England and fifteen years later had purchased the splendid Wood Norton estates. Evesham folk were delighted and considered it a great honour that the French aristocracy should choose to live near them. The ornate entrance gates still exist and can be seen from the A44, west of Evesham and about a mile from the town. Locals may know it better as the BBC centre, since it was acquired by the corporation in 1939, but it is now a hotel and conference centre. By 1889, the original owner had died and the estate had passed to his great-nephew, the duc d'Orléans.

Verdant and well-tended acres such as these were overrun with rabbits, pheasants, pigeons, ducks, even deer, and all manner of edible livestock, attractive to both the poor, who were struggling to survive, and those of dubious reputation who were keen on making a quick penny or two – small wonder that a fifth of all the crimes to come before the courts were associated with poaching. During the 1800s this was regarded as a more serious crime than theft. Poachers could be transported or imprisoned for up to seven years. Landowners employed gamekeepers or 'watchers' to patrol the land and guard it from poachers.

One of the gamekeepers for the duc d'Orléans was 25-year-old Frederick Stephens. He had lived in Evesham all his life and now rented a cottage at Lenchwick. He had been married about eighteen months and had one small son.

The Boswell Family

In various houses in the centre of Evesham lived the Boswell family, who frequently augmented the family stews and their incomes with a few illicit birds or animals. In those days families tended to be large, and this one was no exception. George, the eldest, was 50 at the time of the murder, then came Eli, Samuel, Joseph, John and James. One girl, Mary Ann, was born after Samuel. Only George could read. The sons prided themselves on their pugilistic skills and hired themselves out professionally during elections to beat up any opposition. They were a family to treat with respect.

Merstow Green, across the road from the Almonry. Samuel Boswell lived in one of the houses here.

Littleworth Street, now known as Littleworth, where Joseph Boswell lived.

The two brothers who were involved in the murder were Samuel and Joseph. Samuel was the older at 37 years of age. He lived in Merstow Green (opposite the Evesham Almonry) with his wife and five children, who ranged in age from six months to nine years. Samuel's life of petty crime began when he was only 16, when he was charged with stealing a hat. He joined the army but after deserting twice was discharged with ignominy. Though Samuel had his faults, he was an affectionate father and looked after his family well. His wife never found it necessary to go out to work.

Joseph was 29 years old and lived in Littleworth Street. The Press later described him as having 'an unprepossessing appearance' with a habit of lowering his head and glowering under bushy, overhanging eyebrows. Frequently charged with minor offences such as drunkenness, trespass and assault, his only serious crime had been four years previously when he was imprisoned for a month for stealing a pair of boots. Again, he was a good family man, and even after having four children he and his wife still adored each other. Although the youngest was still a babe in arms, his wife sometimes earned a little extra money by gardening. Both brothers gave their occupation as 'labourers'.

The Fatal Affray

On the evening of 9 September 1889, Joseph and Samuel were in and out of the *Jolly Gardener*, a public house in Bewdley Street. They were joined by a younger brother, 25-year-old James, who left some time between ten and eleven. A friend of theirs, Alfred Hill, usually known as 'Lovely', was also present.

The younger brother, James, lived near the *Jolly Gardener*. That same evening, a neighbour dropped into the household for a drink and a chat. Both James and his wife were there but not their dog, a brown and white animal, later described as looking rather like a lurcher, a popular hunting dog. However, the neighbour had seen their friend Lovely going in the direction of Joseph's house and he had a dog with him. The dog was kept in an unlocked outhouse and often collected by Samuel, Joseph or Lovely.

Some time that evening, Joseph called in to see James and asked if he was going to have a 'run out'. James said not;

Bewdley Street, home of James Boswell. All three brothers lived within a few minutes' walk of each other.

Joseph swore and left. By the end of the evening, James was the worse for drink and went to sleep in a chair with his head resting on his arms on the table. His wife locked the back door and went up to bed. Later, she heard a great clatter and came downstairs to find James on the floor and the chair broken. He had fallen off in a drunken stupor. She removed the broken chair from under him and went back to bed.

About a quarter to eleven, a neighbour heard the sound of crying coming from Joseph's house. She went to investigate and found the four children left alone in their bedroom. Two of them were crying. She brought the baby downstairs, wrapped him in a shawl and went to look for his parents. Joseph's wife had evidently been to visit her mother, as she was coming from that direction. Joseph was nowhere to be seen.

Meanwhile, the gamekeeper, Frederick Stephens, was patrolling the grounds with a fellow gamekeeper. Their tour began at nine o'clock from the home of the head gamekeeper, Benjamin Wasley who lived near Lenchwick crossroads. About 500 yards from Lenchwick coppice was a wooden house, presumably some kind of hide. They stopped there for twenty minutes, then went almost a mile north to Hipton Hill and west to Craycombe Bank, near the home of the second gamekeeper. They stayed there for two hours then went down south on to the Evesham Road and back up to Lenchwick. Frederick pulled out his watch and announced that it was two o'clock: their shift had finished. His colleague went home to Craycombe Bank and Stephens set off through Lenchwick coppice to his home nearby. It was said later that this was not the most direct route home and he must have decided to continue his tour of duty. The coppice was popular with poachers since it was inhabited by all kinds of game.

Summer was over and there was a nip in the air. Although there was a bright harvest moon the wood was a mass of dark shadows. Suddenly, he heard a rustling in the bushes about twenty or thirty yards away. Coming towards him through the undergrowth were three burly men. Each of the men had a bag and they had two dogs with them, one was light coloured and the other could have been a lurcher.

One of them (Lovely) was shooting at a pheasant with a catapult. Stephens advanced towards them. He recognized Joseph as a member of the Boswell family. Joseph spoke first and swore. He said, 'Let the b … have it!' Their pockets were full of stones and they began throwing them, but none of them hit the gamekeeper.

Apparently, Joseph knocked Stephens down with his fist and struck him in the chest. As Stephens fell, he took Joseph with him. The gamekeeper had the poacher's finger between his teeth and was biting it almost in two. The poacher was throttling the gamekeeper (Joseph later said he had to do this to make Stephens release his finger). Joseph managed to get five net pegs out of his pocket and hit Stephens across the mouth with them. The other two poachers were kicking wherever they could get a boot in. Stephens managed to get to his feet, but a blow with a stick sent him reeling again. Joseph later said that Lovely brought a club down on Stephens's head with all the force that he could muster. Stephens lashed out with his stick but only managed to hit one of them – this may have been when Samuel received a nasty blow to his eye. Stephens was now on the ground, where the three men kicked him in the head and shoulders until he was senseless.

Lovely said, 'Come on, we shall have some more after us.' They raced through the shrubs and across the fields to the Evesham Road, leaving Stephens for dead.

But Stephens was not dead. He regained consciousness and managed to stagger roughly 700 yards to the house of Benjamin Wasley, his face, head and neckerchief covered in blood. Mr Wasley put his horse in the trap and drove Stephens to Mr Haynes's surgery in Evesham. While he was getting the horse ready, Stephens described the attack. Mr Haynes was a member of the College of Surgeons and had practised in Evesham for twenty-five years. Stephens's face and neck were badly bruised and he had two cuts to the side of his head. Mr Haynes dressed the wounds and sent Stephens back home to rest.

Stephens was well enough to give an account of the affray. Joseph was taken to his bedside for identification. James was also taken along as he owned a lurcher that matched

Stephens's description of one of the dogs. Stephens recognized Joseph because they went to the same school, but he had not known his Christian name. He did not, of course, recognize James, who was not involved.

Word soon reached Evesham police station about the attack. At half past three early that morning Police Constable Brinton decided to pay a visit to Littleworth Street. He saw Joseph looking out of his front door, the door was closed, then Joseph looked out again. PC Brinton casually sauntered over and asked him, 'What brings you up so early?' Joseph said he had been drinking. He had fallen asleep on the settee and had just woken up. PC Brinton then asked for a match. When Joseph felt in his pockets the constable noticed the damaged finger and asked, 'What have you done to your finger?' With that, Joseph went into his house and slammed the door, but it was not on the latch and the constable easily pushed it open. He was just in time to see a figure disappearing out of the back door. Joseph called to PC Brinton, 'You can come in now.' A brown and white dog rushed at the constable barking furiously, but Joseph held it off with his staff. 'Who was that going out of the back door?' asked the policeman. 'Nobody,' was the reply.

PC Brinton then said, 'Let me look at your shoes.' Joseph handed him a dry pair which had obviously not been worn for some days. The constable said, 'These are not your shoes.' Joseph shouted 'Yes they are!' and began raving and shouting, 'Where's your search warrant? You shall not search my house! Get out of my house!' His wife heard the noise and came downstairs, asking, 'Whatever is the matter?' Joseph said that if the constable didn't get out of the house, he would knock his b... head off.

The noise woke one of the neighbours, who looked out of his bedroom window, just in time to see Sam, Lovely and Sam's wife outside Joseph's house. Sam was told to get over the wall 'or you will be took'.

A Tragic Conclusion

Princess Helena d'Orléans paid for a trained nurse to sit with Stephens and the comtesse de Paris, who happened to be staying at Wood Norton, visited the little cottage at Lenchwick twice a day.

Frederick Stephens
10 March 1864-
23 November 1889

Fred Stephens.

At first Stephens's injuries were not thought to be life-threatening, and for the next two days, even though he was drifting in and out of consciousness, he was thought to be improving. Two days later he began to be drowsy. By 15 September he had lapsed into a coma. It was obvious to Mr Haynes that he was suffering from compression of the brain. Having decided to operate, when Haynes opened the scalp he discovered a small piece of broken skull. With limitless resources from the d'Orléans's purse at his disposal, he decided to telegraph two eminent brain surgeons in Birmingham. At the next operation a piece of skull the size of a fist was removed and a slight rupture was evident in the covering of the brain. The strange thing was that, although there were cuts and bruises to the skull, these were not in the same place as the fractures. Again, the patient seemed to be improving for a few days, then on the Sunday he began to suffer convulsions. The following Wednesday he became lethargic and drowsy and drifted into unconsciousness. On Friday, he rallied a little, recognized his wife, then on 23 November 1889 he died. At the post-mortem, Haynes discovered that the fracture was five inches in length and Stephens had another fracture going backwards over his left eye. Haynes said it was amazing that a man with such serious injuries should show such minor symptoms. He said that the fractures could have been caused by blows from a stick or from kicks with boots.

The whole village mourned. All blinds were drawn and most of the villagers wore some sign of mourning, such as a black armband. Three days later, mourners sobbed as Stephens was laid to rest in Norton churchyard. The duc d'Orléans lent one of his coaches for the widow and other close relatives.

This tragic event provided local men of the cloth with topics for sermons for many weeks. Perhaps the most interesting came from the mayor who spoke from the pulpit of Evesham Wesleyan chapel. He said he had been acquainted with one of the accused since childhood. He had been a kind-hearted and sensitive lad but 'get a man under the influence of drink, and all those impulses which used to be regarded as something noble and amiable became brutalized and blunted, and perverted to the basest purposes.'

Assaults on gamekeepers were common. Two days after the affray at Wood Norton, for example, two gamekeepers, father and son, disturbed two poachers at Llanelli in Monmouthshire. When the father seized one of the poachers, the other poacher attacked him with the butt of his rifle. The rifle went off, killing the poacher and dangerously injuring the gamekeeper.

Splits and Squabbles

At nine o'clock on the Sunday morning, the day after the fight, James was still in bed, sleeping off the drink. The back door opened and in crept Joseph Boswell. He closed the door behind him and said to James's wife, 'God bless you, don't split but we b ... nigh killed the gamekeeper.' He described the night's events to her. He said that he wished he had not done it as he only had four rabbits.

A week later, when Stephens had taken a turn for the worse, James's wife reported this conversation to the acting sergeant. The police had only to look at the Boswell brothers to see the evidence. Joseph had a damaged finger and Sam had such a black eye he could hardly see.

Meanwhile, inspection of the site revealed tracks made by three men and two dogs, confirming Stephens's account. Blood was everywhere, on the floor and in the bushes, together with signs of a struggle. Stephens's hat and stick were there, together with five net pegs. These were about thirty inches long and used by poachers to hold up the net for the catching of game. One of the pegs had light-coloured hair sticking to it, matching the colour of Stephens's hair. A blue handkerchief was found nearby. It so happened that a few months beforehand, Lovely's wife had been seriously ill and James's wife had done his washing for him. She was therefore able to identify the blue handkerchief as belonging to Lovely.

A magisterial session was held, then an inquest, which was adjourned for a week. The court at the inquest was so crowded that the magistrate turned everyone out and instructed the bench constable to admit only those with an interest in the case. The constable pointed out that it was impossible for one person to control so large a crowd, but he evidently managed because finally the courtroom was comfortably full and the inquest could begin. Only about a tenth of those waiting had been admitted. Samuel and Joseph looked scruffy, down-at-heel and ill at ease. They fidgeted, hung their heads and seemed cowed and apologetic.

Because three men were involved, the police at first suspected three brothers and so James was put on bail. In court, he was called twice and failed to appear. After the third call there was silence for several seconds, then the courtroom door opened and in walked a tall, good-looking, well-dressed young man. A gasp went through the courtroom. He seemed to be totally unlike his brothers. He spoke clearly and with self-confidence. He gave the impression that he was far too superior to be involved in such a sordid issue.

Joseph told the court:

We started throwing things at him. I catched him by the shoulders and got him to the ground. He then rose and struck Sam a blow in the eye. Lovely struck him with the 'cosh' and he fell down. I fell with him and he got hold of my finger and bit it. I had 'most to throttle him to get him to loose my finger. I drew some pegs from my pocket and hit him four or five times across the mouth. Sam was kicking him at the time. We left him for dead.

Joseph also added a significant statement: 'You ain't got the right 'un who gave him a smack that coopered him if he is dead, sir.' The chairman repeated, 'You deliberately say that we have not got the man that struck the final blow?' Joseph repeated, 'There was but one blow struck and that was all, sir. It was neither of them sticks (pointing to the sticks held in court). It was a bigger one with a knob on it. Lovely leaned over me and struck him as hard as he could on the head. All I did was hit him with my fist. I got up and said, "Good God, you have killed him".'

The courts saw much squabbling between the brothers, their wives and various neighbours, especially between Joseph and James's wife. One statement stood out. Thomas Spragg, a gardener's labourer, was in the *Jolly Gardener* for most of the evening of the murder. He said that at ten to nine, Joseph was in the kitchen of the pub, drinking beer. Samuel came in soon after. Samuel asked Joseph if he was ready. The one said, 'and let any b … come and we will knock his b … head off'. That tallied with the remark heard by Stephens at the beginning of the fight: 'Let the b … have it!' The jury were impressed.

Because of his wife's testimony, corroborated by the neighbour, James was eventually freed. He had to make his way through the crowd to get home. The crowd parted to let him through but everyone stood in complete silence. Only his little dog was pleased to see him, running up to his master and barking with delight.

The Flight of Alfred Hill

Alfred Hill, or 'Lovely', was 23 years old and the youngest of ten children. His family was rumoured to be quite respectable, and in their opinion Alfred was a fine young lad until he fell under the influence of the Boswells. They seemed to have overlooked the fact that his first conviction came when he was only about 13, for stealing toys from a shop. Later convictions were for stealing fruit and vegetables and being drunk and disorderly. He found conversation difficult, his vocabulary was basic and sentences were constructed with the aid of a range of blasphemies. His wife was a slim young woman with one child. He owned a dog, said to be of a yellowish colour, no doubt the dog seen in the affray. For fifteen months before the murder he had been working at a market garden in Bewdley. His employer described him as an excellent worker, never wasting time chatting to his workmates.

Lovely had been sitting in the window of the *Trumpet* in Merstow Green when Joseph was arrested. Very drunk, he went

The Trumpet, *still in Merstow Green.*

into the club room, where there was dancing, and boasted that he knew all about the incident with the gamekeeper and that the police had the wrong men. He therefore more or less confessed to striking the fatal blows. When officers arrived to arrest him he had gone up the yard, presumably to the lavatory. His friends went to warn him. They took him through the stables and through a hole in the rear fence where a friend heaved him over a high wall. By walking along the walls, he was able to drop into the courtyard where he lived. He asked his wife to give him some money so that he could bail out James. Both Lovely and the money then disappeared. He was last seen heading towards the station.

The hunt was on for 'Lovely', Alfred Hill. The police issued a description of him as a gardener's labourer, aged 23, height five feet five inches, fresh complexion, hazel eyes, light hair, slight light moustache, round full face, high cheek bones, tattooed ring ringer on his left hand, left arm and shoulder, bow-legged with strong, thick-set figure, dressed in a grey jacket, dark cord trousers, black soft bullycock hat, and strong lace-up boots. He wore his hat forward over his eyes and had a sullen, downcast look, habitually using low, coarse language. When he was drunk he would sing 'Don't put my father's picture up for sale'.

The duc d'Orléans's head gamekeeper, Benjamin Wasley, had a brother in the police force, a superintendent, who had been transferred to Kings Heath. He took a special interest in the case and made sure that Lovely's description was forwarded by telegraph across Birmingham.

There are two accounts as to how Lovely was caught; perhaps both contributed to his capture. The most interesting version is that the police were asked to look out for any person including the above song in his repertoire. A man was heard singing the song in Dartmouth Street, so the police began to search that area. Another version is that Mr Charles Grove, who lived in the market place at Evesham, travelled by train to Tewkesbury fair. At Ashford, two other gentlemen came into the carriage. They were discussing the murder and the flight of Hill, when the second gentleman said, 'I know where he is, he's working for the corporation in number eight yard.' He had heard this from a friend who was the foreman of the yard.

Back in Evesham, since he had been to school with Lovely and consequently would recognize him, Constable Bayliss was despatched to Moor Street police station. Early the next morning he put on a boiler suit and blackened his face to look like one of the workers. He recognized Lovely and tried to grab him, but Lovely was not to be taken so easily and put up a fight. Luckily two other officers were hiding nearby and ran to Bayliss's rescue. Lovely had been working as a coke runner at Windsor Street gasworks under the name of George Hale and living quietly at 107 Dartmouth Street. His landlady had become quite fond of him, and he was very good with her children. She nearly fainted when she heard that he was wanted for murder.

In the week of 21 February 1890, a grand jury found a true bill against Joseph Boswell, Samuel Boswell and Alfred Hill for the murder of Frederick Stephens. The jury went out at one o'clock and everyone expected a speedy verdict. The court waited, and waited. One of the jurors would not agree that all three were guilty and it took the jury three hours to reach a verdict.

A Tragic Finale

A petition of over 2,000 signatures was organized for the reprieve of the prisoners and sent to the Home Secretary. Had there been one fatal blow and, if so, who had given it? There was some doubt that the foreman of the jury had acted properly during the trial, and, furthermore, if the men were sentenced ten young children would be fatherless and without support.

The two brothers dictated affectionate letters to their wives. Lovely was able to write with difficulty; warders said that his handwriting was like that of a 10-year-old. On 6 January he penned the following touching letter:

If so be that God spare my life to see the wide world once more you will find me a different husband, for this as learned (taught) me your word (advice) which you used to say 'I would (should) not go out tonight'. I think of it many times in a day: that don't make it no better. I will trust to the Lord Almighty to see me through my troubles.

On Saturday, 8 March, fifteen members of the Boswell family took the train to the prison to see the condemned men. Among them were two older brothers George and Eli, two younger brothers John and James, his wife and five children, and his father. Mr Boswell senior was a widower, an old man 'bowed with age'. He was unable to hold back his tears and cried all the way from the prison to his home in Evesham.

Before his family left, Samuel told them that it was Lovely who had given the gamekeeper the fatal blow on the head. He asked them, 'Would I tell a lie with my last words?'

Some of Lovely's family also went to see him. His father, too, was old and overcome with grief, while his wife sobbed bitterly all the way home.

Such a large collection of strangers walking through Worcester, weeping and crying, caused a great deal of interest and concern.

Local hostelries took in various members of the Boswell family and fed them. The licensee of the *Berkeley Arms*, Mrs Cookson, had collected thirty-five shillings for Lovely's family and now she entertained them in her hostelry.

About 8 March 1890, Mr Berry, the executioner arrived. Never before had three men all been hung at once. The pit, which had been built for Moses Shrimpton (see Chapter 9) had to be enlarged. Three nooses were positioned in a row over the pit.

An Astonishing Development

The day before the hanging arrived, 10 March. All three men were prepared for their fate, when suddenly and unexpectedly news arrived that the Home Secretary had studied the petition and one of them was to be reprieved. Everyone was amazed to hear that it was Lovely, the one man accused by the Boswell brothers of striking a fatal blow.

Before the executions a special service was held in the chapel. The condemned men's pew was reached by a side corridor and curtained off, so that they were not visible to the other prisoners. At a quarter to eight the prison bell began to toll, reverberating throughout the prison. Berry visited each of the two prisoners in turn to tie their hands in front of them. White caps were put on their heads and pulled low over each forehead. Samuel and Joseph were each in a cell at either end of a long corridor; they now came out into the corridor and walked towards each other. This was the first time they had seen each other since the trial. Flanked by their warders and followed by a small procession of dignitaries, they walked in procession along the open walkway to the wheelhouse. The gallows were held in a special walled room. Outside these doors, the white caps were pulled down over the faces of the prisoners, and they were led inside. On the floor, under the noose, were chalk marks where the feet should be placed. An empty noose hung between them.

Samuel half fainted and had to be lifted into place. He groaned loudly throughout the chaplain's reading of the burial service for the dead. Joseph startled the onlookers by calling out through his white mask, 'Lord have mercy on us.' Samuel replied, 'Christ have mercy on us.' Joseph called out, 'Oh my poor dear wife and my poor dear children!' They called a 'goodbye' to each other. Samuel added, 'God bless you my boy.' Joseph replied 'I hope everything will be alright.' Those were their last words.

At five past eight a crowd of over a thousand waiting outside the prison saw the black flag hoisted skyward, fluttering in the wind. Many waited in silence until the last toll of the prison bell had died away.

The Boswells' death left nine children without any form of income. The Evesham Guardians had ruled that outdoor relief should not be given to families of bad characters, but that the accommodation of the house should be offered. Joseph's wife went to live with her widowed mother. Samuel's wife was in the worst predicament since she had five children, the youngest being only a few months old, and she had never worked. She had no experience of supporting herself in any field.

There was much bitterness among the relatives against Spragg, who had repeated to the jury the conversation between the two brothers before they set out on that terrible night. Samuel and Joseph said that no such conversation had taken place, and they blamed him for their conviction.

The duc d'Orléans made provision for Stephens's small son. In 2000, just over a hundred years after his murder, Stephens's grandson, Mr W A Stephens, compiled a book about the murder, *The Wood Norton Murder*, published by the Vale of Evesham Historical Society and available from the Evesham Almonry and Tourist Information Centre. It contains a great deal more information than has been included in this chapter. Why not read it and decide for yourself whether Lovely alone should have been reprieved?

CHAPTER 13

Massacre of the Innocents – Severn Stoke, Near Upton-on-Severn

Each account of a murder in this book is a tiny cameo of that period in time, and a reminder of how much life has changed over the past few hundred years. There have, of course, been tremendous advances in technology. The local surgeon no longer arrives at the site of the murder on horseback; it is now the pathologist who drives there by car. The arrival of DNA might have solved at least two of these cases. Life is now more sophisticated. The body is no longer housed in a nearby barn, nor the inquest held in the local public house. Attitudes, too, have changed. This is especially so with regard to sex, which was a subject that used to be

The old Bishop's Palace, near the cathedral in Worcester.

brushed under the carpet and never, ever mentioned. Many a young girl was wed without knowing the facts of life. The author has two friends who came into this category as late as the 1950s. Sex within marriage was just about acceptable, but even then the woman was supposed to open her legs and think of England. Sex outside marriage was totally unacceptable. It was a terrible sin. The girl who bore an illegitimate child was in terrible disgrace. Bastards were blighted for life. If a girl found that she was pregnant it was total disaster. There are accounts of young girls dying from botched abortions, of giving birth in secret and handing the newborn over to a relative or for adoption, and even, as a last resort, murdering the child at birth.

This once happened right under the nose of the Bishop of Worcester. In 1836 the bishop had two palaces, Hartlebury Castle and another a few yards from the cathedral at Worcester; both are still in existence although the Worcester palace was sold many years ago. In July 1836 the bishop brought in some of his staff from Hartlebury to Worcester in preparation for the Autumn Music Festival. Among them was Charlotte Groundsell, who had worked for the bishop at Hartlebury for nine years. She was unmarried and no one guessed that she was pregnant. Sleeping in the same room as Charlotte was another servant, Mary Austin, who was woken in the night by loud groans. When it was time to get up, she went downstairs to report that Charlotte was not well, and at nine o'clock took her a cup of tea. Charlotte was sitting on the edge of the bed in great pain. Mary told the cook, who went upstairs and came down again, saying that Charlotte had been delivered of a child and asking Mary to get some baby linen. When Mary returned, the cook said it was too late. The household had been very busy preparing for the reception of visitors at the palace, Charlotte had been worn out and this probably hastened the birth.

Richard Hill, the local surgeon, was sent for. The afterbirth had not come away and Charlotte occupied all his attention for some time. It was obvious that she had given birth to a baby and so, when the danger had passed, he began looking round for the child. Under the bed was a chamber pot and curled up within it was a dead and bloody newborn girl. Across its throat was a two inch gash. The previous evening, Charlotte had asked for the sewing basket, as she wanted to darn her black stockings, and the basket had been on her dressing table.

The father was John Lewis, the bishop's gardener, a middle-aged man with a reputation for chasing the ladies. He was immediately dismissed. The bishop, however, said that he didn't want a cover-up. Charlotte was subsequently sent for trial at the Lent Assizes, but she was acquitted as the jury said there was no evidence that the child had been born alive. She wept throughout the trial and had to be helped from the dock after the verdict.

Occasionally, the skeleton of a newborn child has been discovered. In 1927, a sixteenth-century house on Bear Hill, Alvechurch, was occupied by Dr Dick. He decided to open a doorway leading from a first-floor passage into the attic space. A baby's skeleton was revealed, lying in the plaster. Forensics stated that the body had been in the house for more than fifty years, dating back to the time when the property was a public house. As it could not be determined whether the child had been born alive or dead, an open verdict was returned. The baby was given a Christian burial in the local churchyard. Two days later Mrs Dick walked past the grave and saw that fresh flowers had been placed there, raising the question, was the mother still alive?

Along here is 'the Old House', where the skeleton of a baby was found.

Interestingly, the house had had the reputation of being haunted for many years. Some villagers said that they could hear a baby crying as they walked past, and when they mentioned this to neighbours, they learned that the house was unoccupied. Dr Dick's son recalled that, in 1919, knocking noises were heard coming from the attic, so much so that a colleague who was interested in psychical research was called in, but he only confirmed that the noises were coming from the attic.

The Case of Poor Mary Burford

Mr Godson, the prosecuting officer at the 1832 trial of Mary Burford at Worcester Crown Court, remarked:

> However improbable and unnatural the crime of a mother destroying her own offspring might appear, experience had taught that when a young woman stepped aside from the paths of virtue, she would sometimes, from shame, and perhaps from a mind bordering from distraction, be induced to commit such an offence.

Mary Burford was born in 1809 and was the youngest but one in the large family of a farm labourer at Hanley Castle. As so often with such families, she was put into service. Although she would have been at the beck and call of the family from 6 am to 11 pm with one half-day a week off if she was lucky, she would be learning good manners and be well fed and well clothed.

In October 1830, when she was 21 years old, she changed employers and went to work for Mr and Mrs Burrows of Woodbine Cottage in Severn Stoke, a village on the A38 just over four miles south of Worcester. Thomas Burrows was a saddler and harness-maker in Worcester and his wife had inherited a substantial sum of money.

Mary was a fresh-faced, attractive country girl. Years of obeying orders had destroyed her self-confidence and made her rather shy and timid. Also working for the Burrowses was a handsome young man named John Drinkwater, whose father was also a farm labourer. Mary and John soon became 'an item'. Mary had been working for the family for only eight weeks when

Severn Stoke, a small, picturesque village, where Mary Burford was seduced.

she and John were sleeping together. The inevitable happened, and she became pregnant.

John later told the Press that he didn't know Mary was pregnant. Mary's version, given in court, was that she told John she was pregnant and he said he would marry her, but later he grew very angry when she mentioned marriage and said he would lose his job if Mr Burford knew what he had been up to. Mary said she dared not mention the subject again.

By June she was probably six months pregnant and it became obvious to all that she was putting on weight. Mrs Burrows asked her outright if she were pregnant, which she hotly denied, saying she had dropsy. This is an accumulation of fluid in the tissues and cavities of the body which can result in a swollen abdomen. Dropsy is now rarely encountered, but it was fairly common in the days of low wages and large families, since it was caused by insufficient protein in the diet. It can also be caused by diseases of the heart, kidneys or liver.

Mrs Burrows had her suspicions about this self-diagnosis and paid for her to see the house surgeon of the Worcester Royal Infirmary. The surgeon diagnosed pregnancy, said that the baby would soon arrive and sent Mrs Burrows a note telling her so. Mary again hotly denied the possibility, said it was all a mistake and left Mrs Burrows's employ. Mary was now homeless, jobless and with a baby on the way.

A Friend in Need

While working at the Burrows's, Mary had become friendly with Phoebe Hayfield, who took in washing for the Burrowses. Mary asked Phoebe if she could find her any accommodation.

Phoebe lived at Kinnersley, about a mile south-east of Severn Stoke, with her husband and four young children. The house was owned and occupied by Richard Colwell, a cooper, his wife and two teenage children. Also living there were John Brydges and his wife, Ann. The house was divided by thin brick and lathe partitions so that, as Ann Brydges was to say later, loud conversations could be overheard. A small attic room, reached by twelve steps, stood half over Phoebe's room and half over the passage. Phoebe said that she could live there, and so Mary moved in on 17 August. She earned her keep by sewing.

After she had been there a week Phoebe asked her if she was pregnant. Mary again denied the fact, saying she had dropsy. Phoebe remarked at the trial that the holes of Mary's stays were worn and repaired, suggesting she had been pulling the laces as tightly as possible.

On Tuesday, 15 September, Mary woke up feeling ill. She went down to breakfast but could eat nothing. She said she had a bad cold. At the inquest and the trial she said she had asked Phoebe to come to sit with her:

Kinnersley, a tiny village near Severn Stoke.

Phoebe did not come to see me until two o'clock, when she came upstairs and asked how I was. I told her rather worse than better, and she remarked what a perspiration I was in, and I then asked her to come and sit with me which she said she would as soon as she had given her child its dinner. I wished her to come and sit with me in order that she might find out what was the matter with me, as I did not like to tell her: she stayed about three minutes and went away.

Phoebe said at the trial that she had received no such request. However, two of her friends had a different story. Phoebe had told them both that Mary had asked her to sit with her and she afterwards regretted that she hadn't done so. Perhaps it was unreasonable of Mary to expect a mother of four young children to give her an afternoon of undivided attention.

At the trial, Phoebe said that she had noticed that Mary had lost a lot of weight on the following day but she had no idea why that might be.

The Tiny Corpse

On Saturday night, a terrible smell began to seep through the thin walls, coming from Mary's room. On Sunday morning, when Mary was at breakfast, Phoebe crept up to search her room. The smell came from a box behind the door of her room tied with cord. Phoebe lifted the lid. Underneath was an apron. Phoebe moved the apron and was almost sick at the sight of a newborn baby girl, swollen and gangrenous. The body was lying face down and Phoebe turned her over. A piece of twisted flannel, known as a list, was tied round its neck and stuffed into its mouth. Phoebe fetched Ann Brydges and together they marched down to breakfast to confront Mary.

Phoebe asked Mary why she hadn't come down to breakfast. Mary replied, 'I have had breakfast enough.' Phoebe asked, 'Why, what's the matter?' Mary stated in court that Phoebe had then remarked, 'Now madam, I have you at my option to do as I like with you,' but Phoebe denied saying this. Phoebe wanted to send for Mary's father and sister, but Mary begged them to say nothing. The two women asked her how she did it. She told them that she put a list round the baby's neck and pulled, and stuffed the ends into the baby's mouth.

Phoebe was, of course, appalled. She went to collect some washing from Mrs Burrows and told her about it. Then she went to evening service at the old parish church of St Denys. She told the parish officer, Constable John Tibbet and William Pearce his deputy. All three went to Kinnersley, though PC Tibbet went first on horseback to fetch the surgeon. Mary was examined and it was obvious that she had recently given birth. The county coroner was informed and on Monday, 19 September an inquest was held in the *Boars Head Inn*. Mary was sent to the county gaol to await trial.

The trial was held on 8 March 1832. Despite the fact that cholera was spreading rapidly through the country, the court was crammed to capacity. Mr Burrows dragged John Drinkwater along, but neither of them was called.

Mary was totally distraught and cried throughout the trial. Her attempt to keep her pregnancy a secret had resulted in the whole of Worcestershire hearing about it. She pleaded, 'not guilty' in a weak, tremulous voice. She had had nearly six months to deliberate upon her story and adapt it so that it was more favourable to her plea. She told the court:

> I lay in bed till five when I was delivered of a child, but the pain and agony I suffered at the time of my delivery and for some time after was so great I placed a garter round the neck of the child to help deliver myself with no intention of doing the child any injury. I lay till about six o'clock when Phoebe called me to come to tea. I put the child in a box and came downstairs where I stayed about an hour, then I went upstairs and went to bed. I never heard the child cry or make any noise or stir.

The public prosecutor said that the baby had gone full term and was therefore unlikely to have been born dead. The surgeon said that the dead baby was so swollen and putrid that he was unable to examine her. He could not say definitely whether the list had caused the baby's death, since it might have been placed round the neck to help delivery, though the two combined, the list round the neck and the stuffing in the mouth, would have caused death.

Mary's friends rallied round. Ann Brydges stated that she had been in the house at the time and though the walls were so thin that you could hear anyone in the next room who spoke loudly, she hadn't heard a baby cry. Mrs Burrows described her as a kindly dispositioned, civil girl. A former employer said that Mary was a kind-hearted girl and remarkably fond of children.

The trial lasted for seven hours. Summing up, Judge Littleton said that the jury should consider whether the child was alive at the time of birth and, if so, whether the prisoner caused its death. If, as she stated, the list was put round its neck without any intention of doing it any harm, then they ought to acquit her of murder, and in considering this they ought not to forget the exceedingly good character she had received. If, however, they should acquit her of murder, they should then consider whether she had been guilty of concealment of birth.

The jury took five minutes to decide on their verdict of 'not guilty', stating that they wished to recommend her to mercy. However, the judge said that there were circumstances in the case which would not justify him listening to such a recommendation and he had no option but to give Mary the maximum sentence for concealment of a birth, two years' hard labour. In the 1830s, this *was* hard labour, such as smashing stones to use for the repair of roads.

If Anne and Phoebe's story is to be believed, Mary had confessed to them that she had killed the baby. Yet she told the court it was an accident. However, whichever story is true, one cannot help feeling sorry for her. She was fundamentally a decent, virtuous, modest young lady, swept into a horrendous situation by an affair of the heart. She was a victim of the attitudes of the time.

Bibliography

Bishop of Oxford, manuscript, 'The Truth of the Case. Palmer and Others', undated (accessed at the Family History Centre, Trinity Street, Worcester).

Brown, Alfred W, *Evesham Friends in Olden Times*, West Newman & Co, 1885.

Bund, J W Willis, *An accurate account of the inquest held upon the remains of Richard Hemming, 1830*, T Eaton, College Street, 1921.

Cooper, Margaret, 'Bromsgrove Hospitals', in *Rousler*, Magazine of the Bromsgrove Society, 1986.

Cross, A G R, *Three Early 19th Century Murder Trials*, Severn Stoke Studies, No. 6, privately published, c. 2000.

Davies, Pat and Lorna Sage, *Alvechurch Past & Present*, privately published, 2002.

Eagle, T K, *A Short History of Upton Snodsbury*, privately published, 2006.

Foxe, John, *Actes and Monuments of these Latter and Perillous Days, touching Matters of the Church* (usually referred to as Foxe's *Book of Martyrs*), 1st edn, London, John Day, 1563, page 172.

Hawkins, David T, *Criminal Ancestors – A Guide to Historical Criminal Records in England and Wales*, Sutton, 1992.

Land, Neville, *Victorian Workhouse*, Brewin Books, 1990.

McCormick, Donald, *Murder by Witchcraft*, John Long, London, 1968.

Stephens A W, *The Wood Norton Murder*, Vale of Evesham Historical Society, 2000.

A History of the County of Worcester, Victoria County Histories (1st edn 1926; repr. 1971).

A great deal of the information for this book has come from local newspapers. I would therefore like to thank the librarians at Bromsgrove, Evesham, Kidderminster, Redditch, Birmingham Central Library, Worcester Record Office and especially the Family History Centre in Worcester for their help and guidance.

Every effort has been made to ensure the accuracy of the information presented in this book, but any occasional errors made by the contemporary Press may have been reproduced here.

Index